Nicholas T. Dines

Landscape Perspective Drawing

Cover:
(l) Second stage of
construction of three-point
perspective cube (page 68);
(r) Shadow projection for
three-dimensional simulation
drawing, three-point
perspective (page 88).
Photo: Nicholas T. Dines

Library of Congress Cataloging in Publication Data

Dines, Nicholas T.
    Landscape Perspective Drawing / Nicholas T. Dines.
        p.   cm.
    Includes bibliographical references and index.
    ISBN 0-07-017008-8
    1. Landscape architectural drawing—Technique.   2. Perspective.
I. Title.
SB476.4.D56   1990
712'.3—dc20
                                                    90-62010
                                                      CIP

1234567890   FGR/FGR   9543210

ISBN 0-07-017008-8

*The editors for this book were Joel Stein and Vilma Barr, and the design was by Two Twelve
Associates, Inc., Juanita Dugdale, project manager, and Terrie Dunkelberger and Jose Delano,
project designers. Production supervision was by Business/Professional Editorial Services, Inc.
This book was set in New Baskerville and Univers. It was created electronically by Two Twelve
Associates using PageMaker® 3.2 on the Apple® Macintosh.™*

Printed and bound by Arcata Graphics Company.

*For more information about other McGraw-Hill materials, call 1-800-2-MCGRAW in the United
States. In other countries, call your nearest McGraw-Hill office.*

Landscape
Perspective Drawing

Nicholas T. Dines

McGraw-Hill, Inc.

New York	Lisbon	Paris
St. Louis	London	San Juan
San Francisco	Madrid	São Paulo
Auckland	Mexico City	Singapore
Bogotá	Milan	Sydney
Caracas	Montreal	Tokyo
Hamburg	New Delhi	Toronto
	Oklahoma City	

for Susan, Emily, and Eleni

Table of Contents

Acknowledgements

The basis of this entire book stems from a conversation with Herb Schaal over coffee 20 years ago, when he was an instructor at Syracuse University (he is currently a principal with EDAW, Inc., Fort Collins, Colorado). During the discussion he sketched a one-point perspective depth proportioning system on a table napkin which demonstrated a system of perspective construction that eliminated the need to project from a measured plan. That diagram led me to a woodcut by Albrecht Dürer and other early perspective construction experimenters, which in turn led to my own investigation and experimentation, and eventually to the material contained in this book.[1] Hundreds of students over the last ten years have unwittingly assisted me by allowing me to experiment in the classroom, where their vital questions led to refinements and clarifications.

Landscape Perspective Drawing combines the work of other authors, with some personal experimentation to produce a hybrid of sorts. It is with deep appreciation that I acknowledge the work of: Nigel Walters and John Bromham, authors of *Principles of Perspective*, an extraordinarily concise work on descriptive geometry and perspective theory; Jay Doblin, author of *Perspective: A New System for Designers*, which illustrates short-cut construction methods; and William Kirby Lockhard, author of *Design Drawing*, which has become a classic text and which presents a well-reasoned and superbly illustrated case for using three dimensional drawing as a basis for design exploration and development. To these authors, and to the many others cited in the book, I would like to express my gratitude.

It is with profound appreciation that I thank my friend and colleague, Dr. Nikolaos Kantartzis, Professor of Floriculture and Landscape Architecture at the Polytechnic School in Athens, Greece for providing me a place to work and to live while on sabbatical leave, during which time most of the drawings for this book were prepared. Some of the examples shown were done in collaboration with Dr. Kantartzis for projects in various parts of Greece.

I am also grateful to Dr. Linda Slakey for her editing of early versions of the manuscript, and to Dr. E. Bruce MacDougall for his editorial suggestions for Chapter 9. I wish to thank my colleague, Professor Mark Lindhult, who has been instrumental in stimulating my interest in computer aided design drawing through his research and teaching accomplishments and our numerous conversations.

A special note of thanks is extended to Design Workshop Inc. of Denver, Colorado for graciously allowing me to use the computer simulation images of their work in Chapter 9. Finally, I gratefully acknowledge the elegant work of Ms. Fang Fang who developed, with only minimal instruction, the computer program used to generate the computer space grid images in Chapter 9.

Any creative work depends upon a constellation of experiences and ideas which become fused over time, so that tracing each fragment back to its origin becomes an impossible task. In this acknowledgement, I have attempted to give credit to, and to express gratitude for the direct and indirect assistance that I have received.

Nicholas T. Dines
Williamsburg, Massachusetts

Preface

Designers and artists alike require the ability to mentally conjure three dimensional images, and then to transform those images into perspective drawings or other forms of three dimensional modeling. Each design discipline has a particular point-of-view, and its own palette of elements requiring representation in drawings or models. The book is structured to address the needs of both practicing professionals in the fields of architecture, landscape architecture, and site planning, as well as students in each area.

Landscape architecture requires perspective drawing systems that are able to represent both intimate and vast spatial planes, which can range dimensionally from hundreds of square feet to hundreds of square miles. Many measured perspective systems have been designed to represent objects in spatial settings, such as buildings, automobiles, and appliances. However, landscape architecture often objectifies space per se, and employs "objects" such as buildings, trees, vehicles, etc., to serve as spatially defining and modifying elements, otherwise referred to as context, or "entourage."[2]

Therefore, depicting, or "drawing space" is a prime task for landscape architects and those who frequently do site planning and site design. It is the opinion of this author that the most useful three-dimensional drawings are ones created during the early stages of "form-giving," and are often referred to as "concept" sketches, or the more arcane, "thumbnail" sketches.[3] These early images of emerging ideas can be powerful indicators of a design idea's potential feasibility, character, or contextual compatibility, if the sketches are accurately drawn and interpreted.

The designer in modern practice rarely has the time and/or budget to use measured perspective simply to produce "in-process" sketches which address the spirit of place, or the perceived proportions of space from a potential user's point-of-view; such methods are usually reserved for illustrating fully processed ideas. Computer aided drawing (CAD) provides the capability of creating such early sketch images, using minimum input, but such systems are not yet the rule, and are not yet being used as "design tools" in most office circumstances.[4] Examples of CAD drawings, which are derived from the methods presented in this book, are presented in the last chapter.

The purpose of this book is to present a perspective drawing system which combines the accuracy of measured perspective with the speed and informality of conceptual or thumbnail sketches. This objective is accomplished by combining a number of perspective projection systems and placing them within a pedestrian eye-level landscape environment in one-, two-, and three-point perspective. In addition, aerial views of each perspective type are presented to capture an overall image of a proposed layout, or spatial setting. In the course of researching the documented systems referred to in the text, the author has discovered short-cuts for setting up the perspective drawing, as well as new methods for illustrating landscape perspective theory.

This book assumes that the reader possesses fundamental drawing and drafting skills, but to aid those who are still in the process of acquiring such skills, an annotated bibliography is included to provide additional source material for further study.

Introduction: Drawing Landscape Space

"Perspective is a way of thinking about observation, a method that harnesses and organizes space."[5]

The concept of "harnessing" space using a two dimensional medium establishes a paradox that has intrigued and challenged designers for centuries. The Fifteenth, Sixteenth, and Seventeenth centuries produced an explosive array of theories, books, and drawing "machines," such as that shown in Fig. 3-2. Most of these efforts were aimed at producing "correct" perspective, and tended to enrage the painters of the day, who insisted that their "vision" needed no correction.[6] However, these early experimentations established methods of visualizing the "human landscape," using the human figure to determine relative distance and depth measurements, as indicated in Figs. 2-3, 2-4, and 2-5, and provide the student of landscape design drawing, a source for insights beyond mere technique. The theories explored in this book are drawn from these early works.

Landscape perspective views have historically been used to reconstruct the past, document the present, and to speculate about future prospects. The late eighteenth and early nineteenth century landscape paintings (Constable and Delacroix, for example), are filled with landscape images evocative of both romantic serenity and heroic power. They are characterized by Constable's "pre-impressionist" colors (more vivid than reality), and Delacroix's symbolic escape from the "industrial revolution" through the portrayal of the exotic.[7] Gardens and garden drawings of this period often reflected the same affinity for the "tableux," or the romantic vista, as observed in Paxton's design for Birkenhead.[8]

Unlike the Eighteenth and Nineteenth century examples previously cited, modern landscape design drawing is less concerned with the "tableux," or posed landscape, and more concerned with the dynamics of designed land-scapes and their potential as places for human interaction, habitation, and sense of belonging. In modern practice, designers often create perspective sketches and/or scale models to study the "spatial essence," or "feeling" of a proposed design. However, it is in the perspective drawing that we find the user's point-of-view, especially if a series of sketches "animates" the user's path, simulating movement through space.[9]

Simulating space, movement, and therefore "time," using perspective draw-ing, does indeed require a special "way of thinking about observation." It requires not only the obvious drawing skills needed to represent the artifacts and natural features which define place, context, and space, but also an understanding of basic human visual perception parameters and limits. The designer then has the capacity to "simulate" through drawing, the spatial po-tential of a particular design, and to assess the probability of achieving a given set of "visual objectives." This assessment is aided by a broad range of graphic simulation techniques, all of which support the insights attained through the application of landscape perspective drawing.

Perspective Drawing and the Design Process

The design process, generally referred to as "creative problem solving," is a central link between the related professions of Landscape Architecture, Architecture, Interior Design, Industrial Design, and Engineering. Each of these professions has a unique point-of-view, because each addresses specialized sets of problems for different purposes and at different scales. However, each depends heavily upon graphic means of expression, not only for presenting ideas, but also for generating and assessing ideas. The real "work" of design transforms information (design data) into design forms, and assesses the design ideas as well; the process involves more than mere presentation. Students of design often fail to appreciate the difference between "after the fact" presentation drawings, and "in process" design drawings.

The purpose of this chapter is to illustrate the various design drawing types that are generally associated with design process phases, as indicated in Fig. 1-1. First, it must be stated that the literature on cognitive "problem solving processes" is extraordinarily extensive, and the writings which specifically pertain to architectural design processes are richly varied to include such empirically derivative processes as Christopher Alexander's, *A Pattern Language*, and Jon Lang's more analytical treatise, "A Model of the Designing Process."[10] A balanced description of processes used by site designers is found in *Site Planning*, by Kevin Lynch, and Gary Hack.[11] However, as Lang points out, creative people ..."are notoriously inaccurate"...in their analyses of their own activities; and "there is a substantial difference between the actual design process and the process imagined by most architects."[12]

Design problems in architecture and landscape architecture may be referred to as being "ill-defined," or "wicked," because they are characterized by the occurrence of "unknown-unknowns," which often result in creative solutions that were unpredictable or unexpected at the outset.[13] Simply put, the "great" design often solves problems not originally part of the design parameters, exceeds performance standards, and is aesthetically pleasing as well as functional. It breaks the rules.

■ *The enigmatic aspect of design therefore rests within the designer's inner vision and the capacity to re-assemble fragmentary information into a recombinant whole, and to simulate these visions through drawing and electronic media.*

The process so described is iterative and defies a step-by-step description. However, the drawings, or graphic products of the larger process are describable, and are the subject of this book. To fulfill the needs of this chapter, a simplified process is presented to emphasize typical drawings found in most site planning and design projects.[14]

Fig. 1-1 diagrammatically illustrates a sequence of activities, and identifies factors that influence design decision making. Each of the shaded boxes (1-6) represents a key phase which generates some form of graphic product. The phases do not actually follow the same linear sequence, and many individuals find so much overlap that boundaries are difficult to describe, but the overall diagram does represent a general model structure. While not universally applicable, the following list summarizes these key phases and identifies generic graphic products typically produced by the work in each phase.

1. Problem Recognition and Conceptualization. The problem is identified, defined in light of theory and recent case studies, and conceptualized as a set of variables, visualizations, and data factors which need to be analyzed, or "filtered" through a series of "screens" existing in the problem per se, and the problem context (i.e., site, area, region, etc.). Drawing types produced by this phase are illustrated in Fig. 1-2 as types 1. and 2., which convey verbal, organizational, conceptual, and diagrammatic information, using graphic techniques that reduce the complexity of written material, and which symbolically illustrate fundamental relationships of problem factors (i.e., diagrams).[15]

2. Problem Context Factors and Variables. All elements of the problem as conceived in phase one must be "filtered," or analyzed in terms of the problem context, and given a weighted priority, or value. This phase establishes the basis for form-giving criteria, shapes and directs the flow of thinking, and modifies initial conceptualizations. Drawing types 3 and 4 shown in Fig. 1-2 show programmatic and site diagrams, which often show conceptual sections as well.

3. Preliminary Design. The design criteria implied in (2) are "transformed" into preliminary physical forms which are assigned specific functions, and physical and visual attributes. The design is tied to a specific list of "program elements," which are physically arranged as a series of design "options" for further study. Drawing types 4 and 5 shown in Fig. 1-2 illustrate both diagrammatic and scaled preliminary designs. A "measured site plan," may be interchangeably called a "scaled diagram," for in essence, all scaled plans are indeed "diagrammatic" representations of some real or proposed state.

4. Design Assessment. The preliminary design options must be assessed based upon performance criteria established early in the design process. Additional criteria is often introduced during the design process by "unknown unknowns," and by external review agencies. The design options need to be "simulated," or modeled in a number of ways to assess their validity and to estimate their probability of succeeding. Physical scale models are often produced at this point to gain a three dimensional sense of the proposed final outcome. Drawing types 5 and 6 in Fig. 1-2 represent rendered plans and perspective sketches respectively. Design cross-sections as shown in type 6 add another dimension to plan representations and to perspective drawings as well.

5. Design Development. A design option is selected and refined or altered based upon the design assessment, and fully dimensioned as a pre-construction document. The refinement or alteration stemming from the assessment might require the design to be re-worked, or re-designed as indicated in the feedback loop, resulting in a new preliminary design.

6. Implementation. The design is redrawn as a set of construction documents and the project is supervised and built, occupied, and finally re-assessed in its post-occupancy stage so that new theory and/or experience may be documented and made accessible for the next similar project type. Sadly, this last feedback loop rarely occurs in a systematic manner and therefore built works inadequately inform the design process and the knowledge upon which it is supposed to be based.

Fig. 1-1

Diagram of a cyclical creative design process.

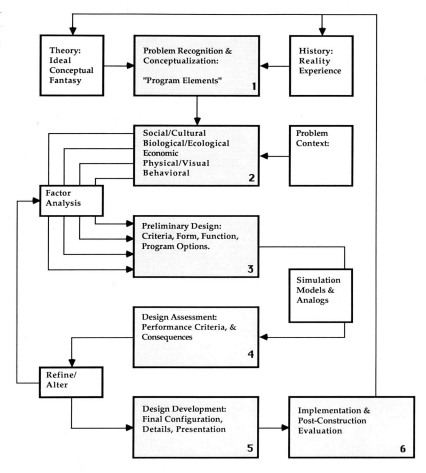

In summary, the process diagrammed in Fig. 1-1 generates the need for four general types of design drawing, three of which are illustrated in Fig. 1-2, and previously described. The fourth type involves the preparation of construction drawings. This book is focused on the third type, namely "two and three dimensional design simulation drawings" in the form of spatial cross-sections, projections, and one-, two-, and three-point perspectives. It is this group of drawings that are crucial to the three dimensional modeling of design ideas, and that are most often difficult for the designer to accurately and efficiently produce.

Fig. 1-2

Illustration of various drawing types produced during the design process:
(1) Organization of verbal concept statements, conceptual models and/or diagrams, or project schedules, etc.;
(2) Statements of design objectives and criteria with illustration figures and diagrams;
(3) Site program and analysis summary diagrams with explanatory text;
(4) Concept or design schematic diagrams showing major program elements and movement linkages;
(5) Design layout showing all program elements, structural and vegetative massing, open space patterns, roads, paths, etc.; and
(6) Descriptive text, perspective, and sectional views of the proposed design (simulation graphics).

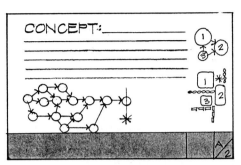
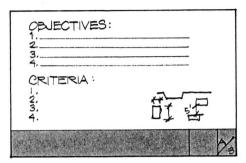

1   2
VERBAL, ORGANIZATIONAL, CONCEPTUAL & DIAGRAMATIC GRAPHICS

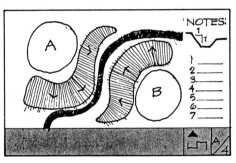
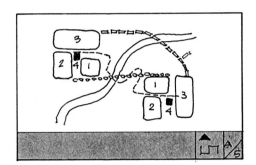

3   4
SITE AND PROGRAMATIC DIAGRAMS FOR ANALYSIS & DESIGN

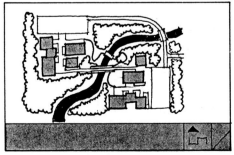
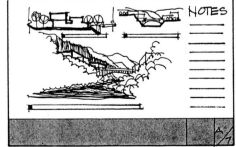

5   6
TWO AND THREE DIMENSIONAL DESIGN 'SIMULATION' GRAPHICS

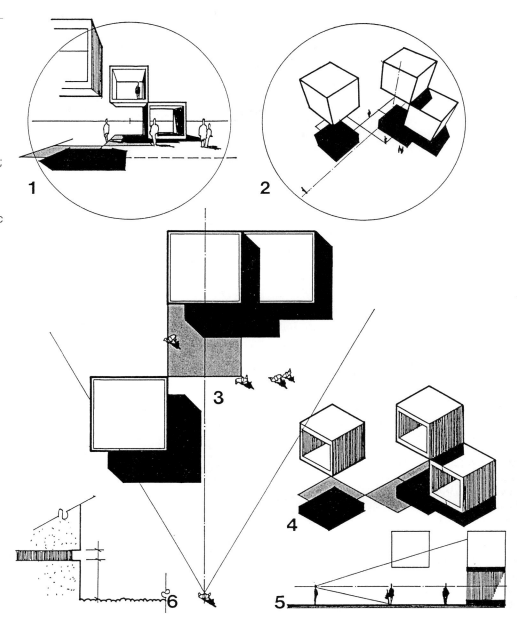

Fig. 1-3

Two and three dimensional visualization techniques for design analysis:
(1) Eye-level perspective view for human scale assessment; (2) Aerial triaxial perspective for analysis of bulk and massing; (3) Plan view, rendered with shadows to illustrate various heights and to study pattern and form (a form of isometric projection); (4) Isometric projections for technical studies in three dimension; (5) Design cross-section views to compare vertical and horizontal relationships, and investigate spatial proportion and human scale; (6) Detail cross-sections to investigate joinery, fabrications, and materials.

Design Simulation Graphics

The designer must develop the ability to think and draw three dimensionally in order to appreciate the true visual meaning of proposed design plans, which as previously mentioned, are merely scaled diagrams that inadequately describe the experiential potential of a proposed design and which require specialized reading skills to translate their symbolic content.

■ *During the course of developing a design concept, it is necessary to envision the proposed design from a number of view points and to express those points-of-view in different graphic modes.*

The six views represented in Fig. 1-3 are ones that experienced designers can view almost simultaneously, in the same fashion that a multi-window computer screen can display a plan, section, elevation, and perspective view of a

Fig. 1-4

Sketch plan of site dimension constraints: This plan summarizes the constraints as set forth by the zoning law and indicates potential opportunities such as the existing trees and topographic features. It also indicates layout dimension criteria which are either determined by the designer, or an external authority. The basis for such a plan is also determined by physical site constraints.

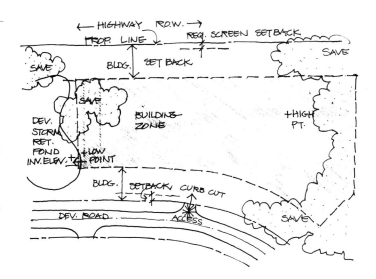

designed object. In other words, when working on a plan, the designer must also visualize a section and a perspective view to give greater meaning to the lines being drawn on the plan, and when drawing a perspective, or section, the plan implications must be visualized.

Sequential Drawing Techniques Applied to Process

Figs. 1-4 to 1-7 illustrate the progression of drawing techniques used in a problem involving the site plan development of a commercial office center from analysis to rendered preliminary sketch plan. The drawing studies do not show all of the drawings required of such a project, but they present in a general way how design drawings express aspects of the design process. Fig. 1-4 is a typical plan diagram meant to organize design data. This particular example has been simplified for illustrative purposes and is limited to zoning setbacks, vegetation cover, basic topographic data, and in an actual case would be comprised of several drawings. Fig. 1-5 is a conceptual diagram

Fig. 1-5

Rough diagrammatic sketch plan of proposed design: After physical and programmatic analysis, a concept plan is laid out on the site without regard to form, to test land area limits and functional feasibility by applying a "model" from theory or past experience.

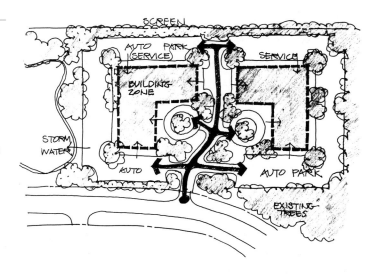

Fig. 1-6

Refined and "scaled" schematic layout plan: The plan configuration is more carefully drawn than in the previous drawing. This plan from the Design Development phase attempts to simulate the actual layout on the site by carefully locating existing trees, property lines, and edges of all pavements within setbacks. It makes design commitments by locating entry points, walkways, planting areas, sign, drop-off area, etc. It represents a form of spatial testing in two and three dimensions;
(1) Schematic "form giving" diagram which interprets the general model
(2) Aerial simulation of volume and mass
(3) Design cross-section to assess planting, grading, and building relationships
(4) Design development base plan for pre-construction purposes

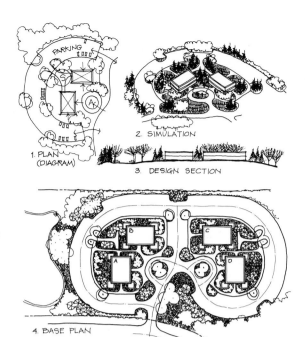

1. PLAN (DIAGRAM)
2. SIMULATION
3. DESIGN SECTION
4. BASE PLAN

Fig. 1-7

Schematic Illustrative plan of the proposed site plan: A rendered presentation plan which shows all major proposed and existing site elements and which indicates depth through the use of shadow projections. This sketch plan is a form of design simulation because it is a scaled reduction of the real site dimensions and is rendered in values to resemble an aerial photograph. It creates the illusion of depth, and therefore implies massing potential (See Fig. 7-11 for a design detail of this scheme).

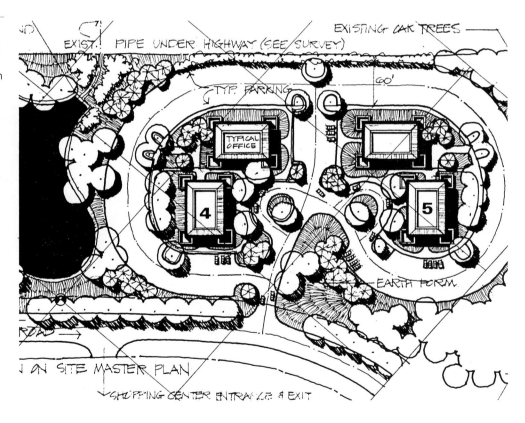

that applies theory and general site conditions to test physical layout feasibility without regard to form. It concentrates attention on program area requirements for gross building and service zones, parking and circulation, overall planting criteria, and preliminary grading and drainage information using spot elevations.

Fig. 1-6 represents the heart of the design drawing process because it embodies "form giving" and spatially interpretive ideas in drawing (1); an aerial "simulation" view to assess massing and general spatial values in drawing; (2) a cross-section to assess grading, planting, and building placement in drawing; (3) and finally, a design development line drawing which summarizes multiple layers of design data, including layout pattern, materials, grading, drainage, and planting in drawing (4). Fig. 1-7 is a typical design development drawing which has been rendered with planometric shadow projections to suggest spatial and mass characteristics. These drawings represent the work required to compare and evaluate a series of proposals for any given site. After evaluation, a modified version of Fig. 1-7 may be developed into construction documents.

Fig. 1-8

One-point perspective as a tool for design and construction assessment: An illustration of how an accurately constructed measured perspective can be used to investigate both two- and three-dimensional design decisions. This sketch also tests such ideas as the proposed tree in the planter, the concrete scoring pattern, the screening effect of the grading scheme, etc.

Fig. 1- 9

Stormwater management "concept sketch":
A freehand aerial view of a proposed residential development drawn during the preliminary design phase to study the open space system as it might relate to a concept of storm water management.

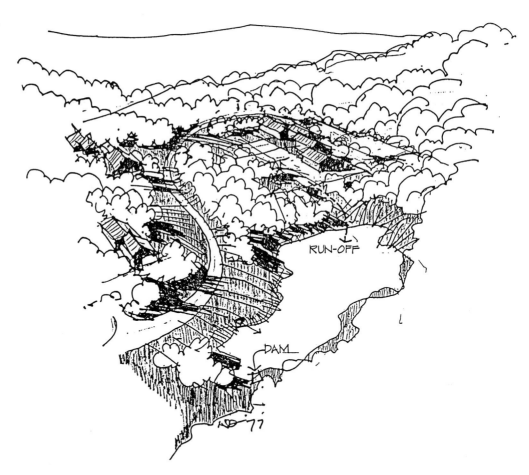

Perspective Studies for Design Assessment

The perspective drawing is a fundamental tool for visualizing the potential spatial effects of a proposed design. Figs. 1-8 and 1-9 illustrate a number of perspective applications to the design assessment process. These drawings are "in-process" images used to evaluate various aspects of site design, and are not intended for formal presentation, although in many instances, such informal sketches can be effective in formal presentations to indicate the "sense" of the design.

2

Landscape Perspective Theory

The most fundamental skill that a landscape architect must possess is the ability to mentally visualize landscape space and time so that designs of almost infinite variety may be constructed, studied, and assessed. This allegorical and, to some extent, metaphorical sensibility is the antecedent of perspective drawing. For the student of landscape architecture, the development of such a skill may be expedited by becoming familiar with general human perception thresholds, and with the visual cues that help to create the expectation and the illusion of perspective space.

If a person standing in a flat open meadow were to gaze in one direction with eyes fixed on the horizon, the person would perceive a scenic landscape perspective view similar to that recorded by a camera. This "fixed" view is essentially what we draw when constructing a perspective. In normal human vision, the head is very rarely held still and erect, and the eyes usually "dance about" the scene being viewed to create a generalized impression of a view much larger than the eyes can perceive at any one moment.

■ *To make sense out of all of this generalized visual information, the eyes seek out familiar objects and combinations of visual phenomena which relate to past perceptual experiences so that meaning can be ascribed to the scenic content.*

These "objects" and visual phenomena are called "visual cues," and are essential to the creation of any perspective illusion.

Landscape Perceptual Thresholds

In landscape settings, for example, it is important to know how far is "far," how close is "close," and how tall is "tall." How far can we actually see discernable objects, interpret the meaning of human activities, or recognize human faces? The answers to these questions are key determinants of both design distances, and of perspective drawing technique as illustrated in Fig. 2-1.

Fig. 2-1 summarizes and illustrates a number of important principles of landscape perspective illusion.

1. Human figures are the most powerful visual cues for establishing perspective depth illusions, because they are entities to which the viewer can most easily relate.

2. Studies measuring perception thresholds have indicated that:

   4000' (1219m) is a distance at which most people are able to visually differentiate human figures from other animate objects such as the cows or sheep which may be roaming in the mythical meadow.

   450' (137m) is a distance at which human activities can be differentiated. (The people in the scene 450' (137m) away from the viewer, for example are parading, not contradancing).

   80' (24m) is a distance at which facial expression is discerned, and explains why good intimate theaters are those which have seats no further away than 75' (23m) to 80' (24m) from the stage.

   40' (12m) is the distance at which familiar faces are recognized.

   20' (6m) is the distance at which objects on the ground begin to enter peripheral vision. In other words, objects or patterns on the ground less than 20' (6m) away cannot be seen unless the viewer's head is tilted toward the ground.

   6'-10' (1.8-3m) is the distance between people seated while engaged in conversation, depending on culture and circumstance.[16]

   3'-4' (1-1.2m) is the distance between people standing and chatting.

3. Any landscape scene can be divided into background, midground, and foreground. In the **background**, colors are pale, warm, and grey, and atmospheric haze tends to "layer" the distant trees, hills, meadows, towns, etc. into generalized horizontal forms which are distinguishable but not sharply delineated. In the **midground**, the colors are more intense, light and shadow

Fig. 2-1

Critical perception depths in the visual landscape:
An illustration of critical perception depths and the minimum components of landscape perspective illusion. The depth planes shown refer to distances from the viewer to the designated point in the perspective. Only the upper half of the foreground figure is visible because the lower half is "outside" of the "cone of vision," and if drawn would result in unnatural distortion and detract from the intended visual cue. Note that graphic representation technique is different in each depth plane, i.e., the tree at the 80' (24m) distance is much more detailed than are trees in the background.

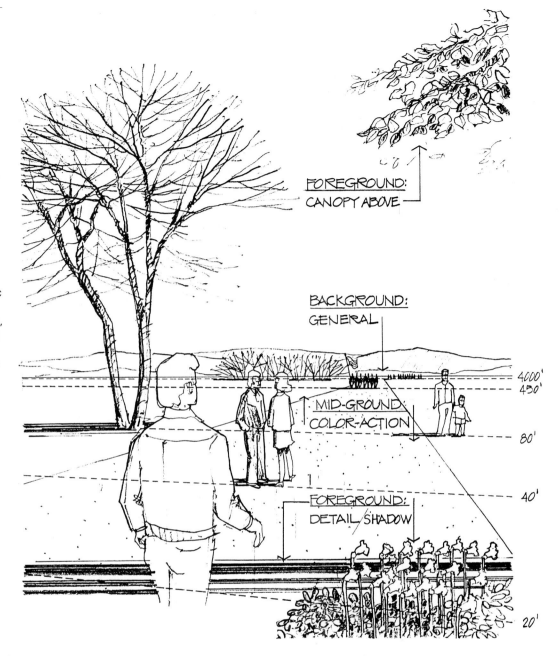

FOREGROUND: CANOPY ABOVE

BACKGROUND: GENERAL

MID-GROUND: COLOR-ACTION

FOREGROUND: DETAIL/SHADOW

4000'
450'

80'

40'

20'

more apparent, and action is more distinct. In the **foreground**, detail, texture, light, and shadow are visually dominant.

4. In landscape perspective illusion, we rely less on "vanishing lines and points" and more upon the layering aspect of landscape forms as they recede into the distance, as well as the juxtaposition of contextual visual cues, such as people, cars, houses, and other structures.

It becomes apparent from Fig. 2-1 that these perception thresholds are important not only for the purpose of understanding how we visually organize the landscape, but also for establishing criteria for selecting appropriate drawing techniques. Simply put, objects drawn in the foreground need to be clear, high in contrast and rich in texture, whereas elements that recede into the background require less distinct delineation. Indeed, if distant elements are drawn too sharply, the results will tend to work against the viewer's natural inclination to generalize such elements as background, thus inhibiting the illusion of depth.

Fig. 2-2

Human figure as a primary depth cue:

People standing on the same plane have a common eye-level of 5' (1.5m). A very primitive illusion of perspective depth can be created by placing figures, drawn at different sizes, and arranged so that their eyes are coincident with a common horizon line (H.L.). Note that each distant figure has a personal depth plane and all have a common eye level.

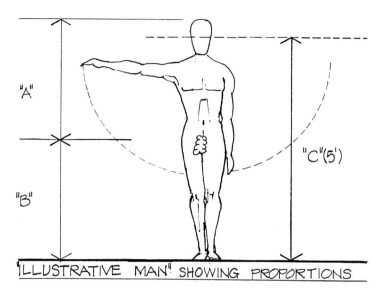

"ILLUSTRATIVE MAN" SHOWING PROPORTIONS

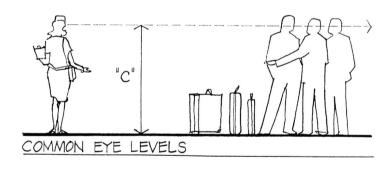

COMMON EYE LEVELS

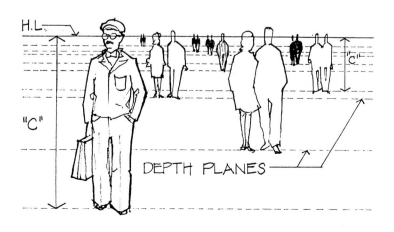

DEPTH PLANES

Human Figure as a Primary Depth Cue

Since the human figure is such a dominant visual cue for distance and depth reference, it is important to study its basic proportions, and the visual dynamics of distributing several figures within a perspective scene. Fig. 2-2 illustrates, for the purpose of drawing, three stylized representations of the human form.

The first, shows a single human figure drawn symmetrically, about the abdomen. The distance labeled "C" refers to a common "eye level" for all human figures who are standing on the ground. For ease of calculation, the human eye level distance is set at 5' (1.5m), which is slightly less than the average real human eye level height of 5'2" to 5'6" (1.6m-1.7m).

The second drawing illustrates the principle of common eye-levels. If people are all standing on the same ground level, it is possible to draw a line which connects or summarizes their common eye-level (horizon line, or H.L.).

The third drawing illustrates the application of this assumption to perspective illusion. If all of the figures shown are said to be standing on the same flat floor level, then even those figures which are far away should have the same eye level. In other words, the viewer, and all of the people shown in this drawing, see the same horizon. Figures so arranged create a primitive illusion of perspective depth, and also serve to illustrate the minimum amount of visual information needed to imply landscape space. They also attest to the sensitivity of our cognitive response to depth and distance cues.

The use of the human figure to reference landscape spatial distance and perceptual cues have a long history in perspective theory.[17] Fig. 2-3 (1576), Fig. 2-4 (1642), and Fig. 2-5 (1800), are historical examples which explore methods of organizing the human landscape, and of exploring perception thresholds.

Fig. 2-3

Architectural construction drawn in 1576 by Jacques Androuet Du Cerceau (c. 1520-after 1584):
Human figures as key scale indicators.

Courtesy of Harry N. Abrams, Inc.

Fig. 2-4

Landscape perspective drawn in 1642 by Jean Dubreuil (1602-1670) using the human figure as the main visual scaling reference:
An early example of an intuitive exploration of human scale and perceived landscape space.

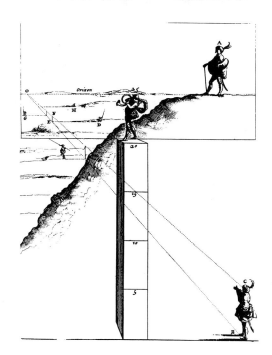

Fig. 2-5

Landscape space drawing produced by Pierre-Henri de Valenciennes (1750-1819) in 1800:
This drawing bears a remarkable resemblance to Figure 2-4.

Courtesy of Harry N. Abrams, Inc.

■ *Landscape perspective drawing exploits the mind's propensity for making sense out of minimal or even extraneous visual information to reconcile visual expectations.*

Fig. 2-6 illustrates in a stylized fashion the essential visual cues of perspective illusion. The upper cross-section view illustrates the horizontal and vertical relationships of a viewer to the landscape being perceived. The viewer on the left, who is always "out of the picture," is standing erect and gazing in one direction past a foreground tree, through an open space, and into a wooded grove. The space and grove are inhabited by other people, all of whom share

Fig. 2-6

The human figure in landscape space:
A presentation of simple perspective illusion created by manipulating scale figures and trees. Note that the roots of the foreground trees are not shown because they are below the cone of vision as indicated in the cross-section view. The perspective view is an interpretation of the section view.

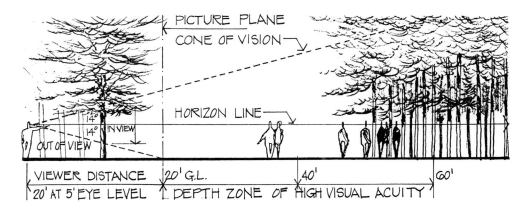

PICTURE PLANE
CONE OF VISION
HORIZON LINE
14°
14° IN VIEW
OUT OF VIEW
VIEWER DISTANCE 20' AT 5' EYE LEVEL
20' G.L.
DEPTH ZONE OF HIGH VISUAL ACUITY
40'
60'

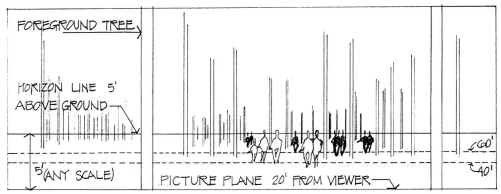

FOREGROUND TREE
HORIZON LINE 5' ABOVE GROUND
5' (ANY SCALE)
PICTURE PLANE 20' FROM VIEWER
60'
40'

LAYOUT OF PERSPECTIVE SCALING ELEMENTS OF SECTION ABOVE

STYLIZED REPRESENTATION: LANDSCAPE SPACE IN SECTION ABOVE

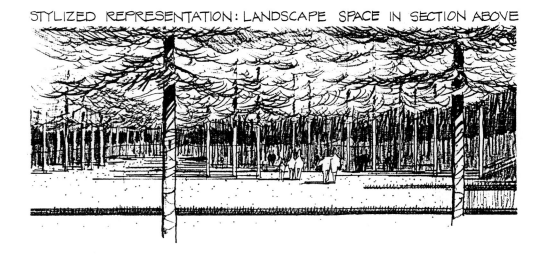

the viewer's eye level; they share a common horizon line reference (H.L.). The viewer, at a point called a standing position or SP, stands in "front" of the scene being perceived. Unable to move the head up or down, or the eyes from side to side, the viewer has a very narrow range of high visual acuity, called the primary "cone of vision." The cone of vision, which is bisected horizontally by the horizon line and vertically by the center line of vision, much like a telescope equipped with cross hairs is divided, limits the amount of information able to be seen at any one time, and "frames" the view in the manner of a picture frame.

The horizontal limit of what the viewer can clearly see is determined by the onset of peripheral vision on the edge of the visual cone. The vertical limit of what can be seen by the viewer is the point at which the top and bottom of the visual cone intersect the ground plane, and roof or canopy plane. The point of intersection on the floor is called the picture plane ground line (G.L.), and is analogous to a large free-standing sheet of glass the size of which has been determined by the cone of vision edges. Since the viewer has a fixed eye level of 5' (1.5m), and a fixed cone of vision of 28 degrees vertically and 30 degrees horizontally, the picture plane will also intersect the ground plane at a fixed point.[18] The geometry of the right triangle formed by the 5' eye level and the bottom edge of the sloping visual cone which is 14 degrees below the line of sight (1/2 of 28 degrees), results in a fixed distance of 20.05', simplified to 20' (6m).

$$\tan 14° = 5'/x$$
$$x = 5'/.249328$$
$$x = 20.0539'$$

Therefore, any eye level landscape perspective view always begins 20' (6m) away from the viewer, and assuming a flat reference plane, all points on the ground, are 5' (1.5m) below the horizon line. The middle diagram in Fig. 2-6 illustrates the application of these observations. The depth lines of 40' (12m) and 60' (18m) are determined by a method described in Chapter 3.

Landscape Space and Interior Architectural Space

There is a fundamental difference between architectural perspective drawing and landscape perspective drawing; the former represents object or mass and tightly defined interior space, whereas the latter represents space or void, within a nearly infinite spatial context. The scale of interior architectural space is fundamentally smaller than the scale of exterior space. Perhaps one of the first lessons learned by a student of landscape architecture is that interior scale dimensions are not applicable to exterior uses because the visual scale references, and human movement behavior, differ profoundly from interior settings. Fig. 2-7 illustrates the importance of spatial context in determining apparent size vs. real size. A 24'x40' (7m x 12m) interior floor area defined spatially by an 8' (2.4m) wall and ceiling is quite generous as an interior space, but when laid out on the ground with no wall or ceiling references, the space apparently shrinks, although such is not the case. So, relative to architectural space, "intimate" landscape space consumes enormous areas in perspective drawings. A landscape distance of 450' (137m) is said to be a normal exterior human scale reference.[19]

In most landscape perspective views, there are many objects which define a space, and which bear no regular geometrical relationship with one another, such as the lake scene illustrated in Fig. 2-8. The critical illusion of depth is being created by overlapping forms and apparent size differences. There is an absence of sidewalk grids, or dramatic line convergence found in most architectural perspective drawings. It is a drawing representing space over the water, with the small building serving as a contextual, rather than principal, feature.

■ *Therefore, the key factor in landscape perspective drawing is understanding relative sizes of various objects at different depths, and employing the correct drawing techniques (line weights, tonal values, etc.) to represent them.*

In so doing, the viewer's visual expectations are met, and perspective illusion readily occurs, without demanding too much interpretation from the drawing viewer.

Fig. 2-7

Comparison of architectural and landscape space perception:
Interior architectural floor area appears to shrink when placed in a landscape context because the scale references are dramatically different (i.e., the sky and horizon).

Fig. 2-8

Landscape scene with numerous "vanishing points":
Landscape perspective represents space and void more than object and mass which results in visual cues quite different from those of architectural perspective.

All perspective views, because they are three-dimensional, have an X, Y, and Z axis, as illustrated in Fig. 2-9. Points on the X axis move left and right relative to the viewer's center line of vision (CV); points on the Y axis move up and down relative to the viewer's horizon line; and points on the Z axis move

Fig. 2-9

Location in perspective by X, Y, and Z co-ordinate points:

All objects or points in a perspective view have calculable X, Y, and Z co-ordinates. The location of people, posts, building corners, trees, even birds in flight, can be accurately plotted in all three dimensions using "measured perspective."

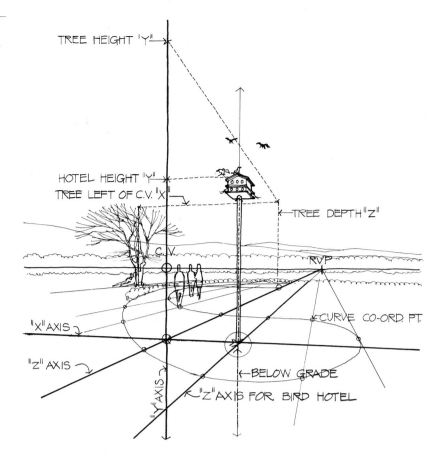

toward and away from the viewer relative to the standing position. In a perspective view, any point can be located by ascribing to it an X, Y, and Z co-ordinate. Drawing systems useful to designers employ elements of descriptive geometry rather than mathematical calculation; in other words, a graphical means for locating points and whole objects in space, or on any plane.

One-, Two-, and Three-Point Perspective Views

One-, two-, and three-point perspective are three major perspective views that are used for both constructing perspectives, and for drawing freehand by visual judgment. Fig. 2-10 illustrates that the three views are determined by the position of the viewer relative to the space or object being viewed. The drawing shows viewers at SP_1 and SP_2 standing obliquely, or at an angle, relative to their center-lines of vision, and to the room being viewed. This oblique viewing angle results in the perspective views SP_1 and SP_2, respectively. The views from SP_1 and SP_2 are called "two-point" perspective because lines such as the corners of wall and floor converge at two different points on the horizon line.

Fig. 2-10

Relationship of viewer position to perspective view:
A diagram of three perspective viewer positions and their resulting perspective views. A three-point perspective has been used to illustrate the aerial view of the three standing positions.

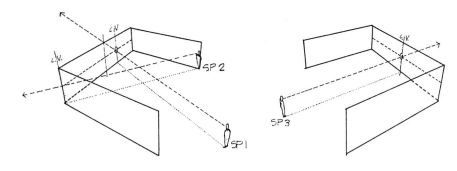

DIAGRAM OF VARIOUS VIEWER STANDING POSITIONS

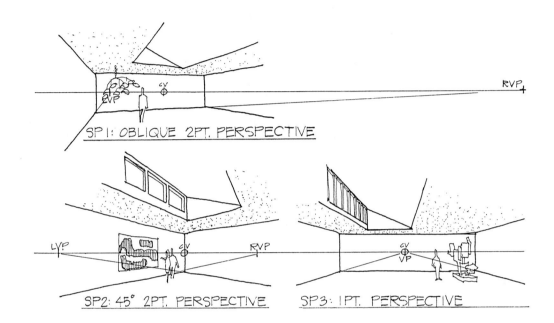

SP1: OBLIQUE 2PT. PERSPECTIVE

SP2: 45° 2PT. PERSPECTIVE   SP3: 1PT. PERSPECTIVE

SP_1 is a common interior two-point perspective view and shows the viewer's center-line of vision (CV) to be about 20 degrees to the right of a line perpendicular to the rear wall being viewed. Another way of expressing this orientation is to envision the room being turned, so that its respective sides are at a 20/70 degree angle relative to the viewer's direction of sight.

The view from SP_2 follows the same principle, but results in a more extreme perspective view because the viewer is focusing diagonally into the far corner. This geometry generates a 45/45 degree two-point perspective.

The viewer at SP_3 is standing perpendicular to the rear wall which creates a one-point perspective view, as shown in the small sketch. In this view, all lines parallel to the viewer's line of vision converge on one point located at the center line of vision (CV).

Three-point perspective is illustrated by the collective view of all three standing positions shown in Fig. 2-10, and labeled, "Diagram of Various Viewer Standing Positions." It is usually an aerial view in which the viewer's head is tilted slightly to look down onto the ground. In three-point perspective, all verticals actually converge to a third point. Note that in the top diagram, the room corners tend to be "slanting" giving the impression that the viewer's head is tilting downward. Chapter 5 will explore three-point perspective in greater detail.

One-Point Perspective

This chapter presents techniques for constructing one-point perspective sketches for both presentation drawings and accurate freehand sketches. The drawings emphasize the structure of measured landscape perspectives. The techniques developed by the author will facilitate speed and accuracy, and encourage the use of perspective sketches during the design process.

Derivation of Depth Scaling

One-point perspective is often referred to as "central perspective," or "parallel perspective" because all lines parallel to the viewer's center line of vision (CV) converge onto one point, located on the horizon line (HL), at the (CV) point. As established in Chapter 2 (Fig. 2-3), the geometry of the cone of vision results in a unique and fixed ratio of vertical and horizontal distances that is the basis of depth measurement.

Fig. 3-1 illustrates the derivation of one-point depth measurement. The upper plan and section of the viewer shows a 28 degree vertical cone of vision and a 30 degree horizontal cone of high visual acuity. A perspective view may be drawn to include a maximum of 60 degrees horizontally, but the main subject area should fall within 30 degrees to prevent unnatural distortion. The bottom sloping edge of the vertical cone intersects the ground at the picture plane, at a rate of 14 degrees and at a distance of 20' (6m) away from the viewer (see Chapter 2). This 1 : 4 ratio of eye level to picture plane distance applies to all one-point perspective sketches drawn within this system. For example, if the eye level height were 10' (3m), the picture plane would intersect the ground 40' (12m) away. Objects on the ground between the viewer and the picture plane occur within the viewer's peripheral vision.

Fig. 3-1

Depth ratios derived from cone of vision geometry:
An illustration of the cone of vision and its relationship to the picture plane (PP), horizon line (HL), and ground line (GL). Depth markers when projected back to viewer, intercept the PP in the manner shown. These ratios are constant for any viewer height.

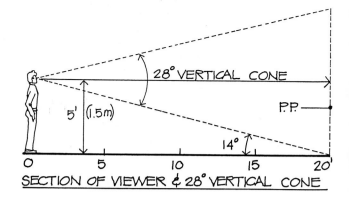

SECTION OF VIEWER & 28° VERTICAL CONE

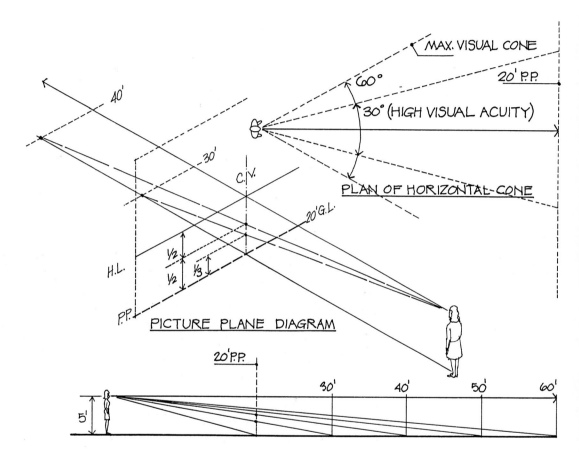

However, any object, such as a tree, which penetrates the visual cone within the 20' (6m) will be seen. The lower diagram in Fig. 3-1 illustrates another result of the fixed ratio of 1 : 4 (vertical to horizontal). Imagine the picture plane to be a large sheet of clear glass, standing perpendicular to a viewer's center line of vision, and upon which is etched a horizontal line (HL) which is drawn parallel to, and 5' (1.5m) above, the ground. The resulting image will resemble the lower diagram and section in Fig. 3-1.

This perspective drawing system places and represents objects and points "behind" the picture plane. The problem to solve for the designer is how to convert depth distances into two-dimensional X and Y locations on the paper, or the imaginary picture plane. The diagrams in Fig. 3-1 illustrate how this conversion for depth is accomplished. The lower section shows a viewer looking off into the horizon, and the space beyond the picture plane is marked in 10' (3m) intervals with metal poles located along the viewer's line of sight. The drawing shows lines, or "pieces of string" running from the viewer's eye-level to the ground markers. All of these projection lines (strings) pass through the picture plane at the vertical extension of the center line of vision, and between the (HL) and the ground line (GL) of the picture plane (PP). It can be seen both in the diagram and lower section that a projection from the viewer to a point on the ground 40' (12m) away passes halfway between the HL and GL; a point 30' (9m) away projects through the picture plane at a point 2/3 of the vertical distance between the horizon line and the ground line (HL-GL), as measured from the HL.[20]   In fact, as shown by the section, the ratios are predictable and calculable, and have been determined to be as follows:

$$30' \ (9m) \ \ = 2/3$$
$$40' \ (12m) = 2/4$$
$$50' \ (15m) = 2/5$$
$$60' \ (18m) = 2/6$$
$$70' \ (21m) = 2/7$$
$$80' \ (24m) = 2/8 \ , \ etc.$$

Fig. 3-2

A 1525 woodcut by Albrecht Dürer:

"Demonstration of Perspective" illustrates the principle of converting depth distances into X and Y co-ordinates on the picture plane.

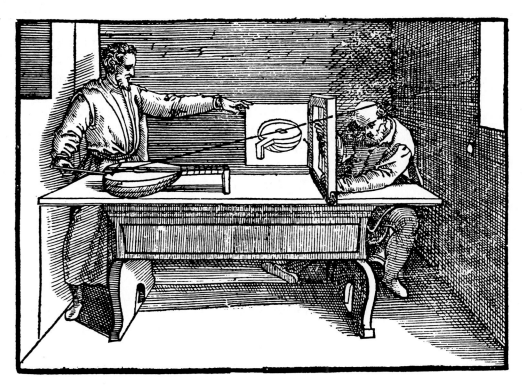

Courtesy of Henry N. Abrams, Inc.

This pattern of fixed ratios is the simple basis upon which the geometry of one-point perspective is constructed. Fig. 3-2 shows a woodcut by Albrecht Dürer in 1525 which illustrates very clearly the conversion of "depth" into a series of X and Y co-ordinates.[21] The person on the left is holding a string and pointing to a specific position on the mandolin, which is analogous to the ground markers in Fig. 3-1. The string passes through a calibrated wooden frame and subsequently through a hook on the wall. The wall hook represents the viewer's eye-level, and the wooden frame represents the picture plane. As the string is moved about the mandolin by the person holding its end, the person on the right measures the X and Y position of the string relative to the frame calibrations, and then closes the wooden door, upon which has been attached a piece of paper, and places a "dot" to represent the measurement just taken. The result is a sixteenth century "connect-the-dot" drawing. It can be clearly seen through the use of this inventive technique that points far away are close to the horizon line with respect to the ground line, and points close to the viewer are clustered about the ground line. In other words, away is "up" and near is "down."

Plan Projection Construction

The traditional method of drawing one-point perspective begins with a plan view, and through a series of projections (the basis of descriptive geometry), a perspective view is constructed. Fig. 3-3 shows this system in simplified form. The plan, drawn to a scale of 1/8" = 1'-0" (1:100), represents a 10' (3m) cube located 20' (6m) from the viewer; its front face is at the picture plane (PP), and its front base edge is on the ground line (GL). The viewer is positioned so that the center line of vision bisects the cube face. From the viewer's standing position (SP), a 45 degree angle is turned and a line extension is projected to intercept a lateral projection of the PP, which in this case is also the cube face. (The 45 degree angle can be projected to either side of the vision center line; left or right has no construction consequence.) Below the plan just drawn, a horizontal line (HL) is constructed, and the center line of vision is projected down, intersecting the newly constructed (HL) and locating the vanishing point (VP). Also, the diagonal vanishing point (45° VP) is projected down vertically to intercept the (HL), which locates the 45° VP at which all diagonals of contiguous horizontal floor plane squares will converge.

■ *In perspective of any kind, all lines parallel to one another, and not parallel with the horizon line, will converge at a single point located on the horizon line.*

Using the same scale as that used in the plan (1/8"=1'-0", 1:100), a 10' (3m) square is constructed so that it is centered on the center line of vision (CV) and bisected by the (HL) to reflect the viewer position in plan, and a 5' (1.5m) eye-level in section. The base of the cube rests on the ground 5' (1.5m) below the horizon line at the intersection of the ground and the picture plane, which is called the ground line (GL). By construction, the cube is 20' (6m) away from the viewer.

Next, the front corners of the cube base are "vanished" back to the VP and projected forward as shown. In other words, a straight-edge is used to connect the VP and the cube base corners, and lines are drawn which pass through the base corners as shown in the perspective view. To construct the horizontal square base of the cube, the 45° VP is employed. A line from the right front corner of the cube base is vanished back to the 45° VP and intersects the previously vanished left front corner of the cube base. This intersection represents a depth distance of 10' (3m) because it is the back corner of the 10' (3m) cube, located by its square base diagonal. Using a parallel bar, the rear edge of the base square is drawn parallel to the horizon line (HL) to complete the square. Using the 45° VP, other squares can be located on the ground and cubes can be constructed, as shown by the 30' (9m) and 40' (12m) cubes.

Fig. 3-3

Plan projection construction of a one-point perspective view:
An illustration of the plan projection method of constructing a 10' (3m) cube which is 20' (6m) away from the viewer. In one-point perspective, the 45° VP is always located on the horizon line at a distance equal to the SP/PP distance between the standing position (SP) and the picture plane (PP) (20', or 6m), or 4 times the eye-level height.

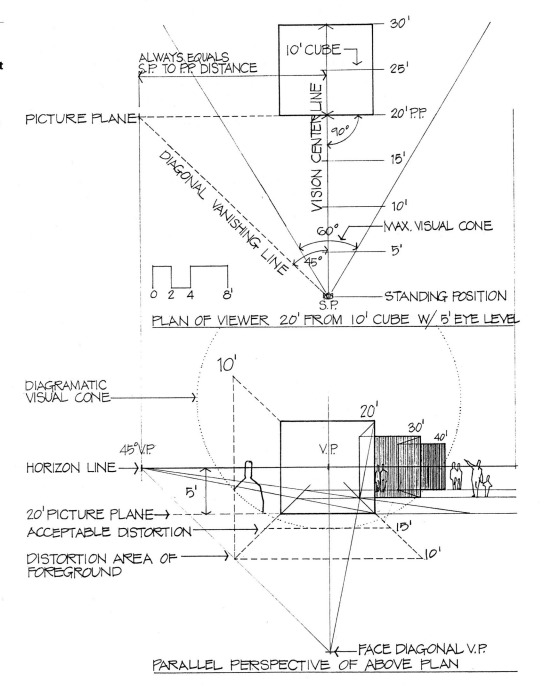

■ *In one-point perspective, a 10' (1.5m) square perpendicular to the vision center line always appears to be a true square, the dimension of which is proportionately reduced by its position in depth. At any depth, given a 5' (1.5m) eye-level, a 10' (3m) square will always be bisected by the horizon line because the base of the square is by definition, 5' (1.5m) below the horizon line.*

The drawing illustrates the extent to which a square is distorted as it is projected in front of the picture plane. The 10' (3m) floor plane square that appears in dashed lines is unacceptably distorted because it is in lower peripheral vision, and in reality is not able to be seen by the viewer, unless the viewer were to scan the scene.

As a general rule for one-point eye-level perspective, objects on the ground should not be closer than 15' from the viewer, because of the distortion that occurs in peripheral vision. Vertical walls parallel to the vision center line all vanish back to the central VP, and the diagonals of all squares located on these vertical walls will vanish to a point located on an extension of the vision center line both above and below the horizon line. This point is referred to in the sketch as the "Face Diagonal VP".

Direct Perspective View Construction

The face square of a 10' (3m) cube in one-point perspective is easily drawn in any depth plane because it is essentially an elevation view of a square, the dimension of which is determined by the "graphic" value of 5' (1.5m) in its particular depth plane. However, depth along the "Z" axis is not so easily measurable because of the perspective foreshortening effect. The key to discovering the actual rate at which distance foreshortens is found in the fixed ratios of depth distances discussed earlier.

Fig. 3-4a illustrates the fact that to draw a one-point perspective view, it is not necessary to construct a plan or make elaborate projections if the principles of such constructions are understood, and can be applied directly. Fig. 3-4a was created by drawing two parallel horizontal lines and labeling the top line HL and the bottom line PP or GL. This construction represents the initial step in constructing any one-point perspective sketch. The distance between the two lines merely determines the size of the sketch. To find various depths in space, it is possible to use any calibrated scale, such as an engineer's scale or a metric scale, and to proportionally divide the space (as shown) to find points on the ground at specifically desired distances from the viewer or SP.

Fig. 3-4

Direct one-point perspective view construction using proportional depth ratios: A system for locating depth reference lines by proportional scaling. By locating the 45° VP as shown, the floor plane can be divided into a grid of 10' (3m) squares.

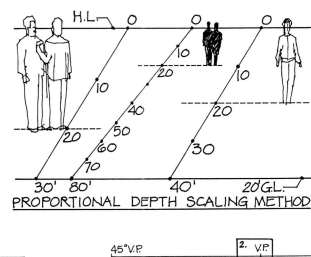

3-4a

PROPORTIONAL DEPTH SCALING METHOD

3-4b

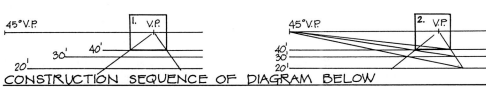

CONSTRUCTION SEQUENCE OF DIAGRAM BELOW

3-4c

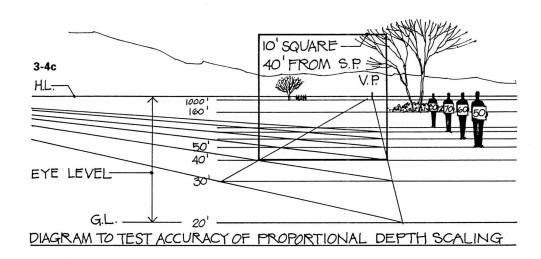

DIAGRAM TO TEST ACCURACY OF PROPORTIONAL DEPTH SCALING

Using the ratios established earlier, distances may be plotted as follows:

1. Place the zero end of the scale at any point on the horizon line and place the desired distance to be located, on the PP Ground Line (G L). (The actual scale used is irrelevant, because the process does not measure, but proportionally divides).

2. Starting at 0, count down 20 (6 for metric) units and place a dot on the paper. The diagram shows this process accomplished for 30' (9m), 40' (12m), and 80' (24m). It soon becomes apparent that in simplified form, we are merely proportionally dividing the space between HL and GL into 2/3, 1/2, and 1/4 proportions; 30' (9m) is always 2/3 the distance from HL, 40' (12m) is always 2/4 or 1/2 the distance from HL, etc. (See Fig. 3-1).

Fig. 3-5

Freehand sketch using depth reference lines:
A freehand application of depth plane divisions by visual judgment. How tall is the tree in the background?

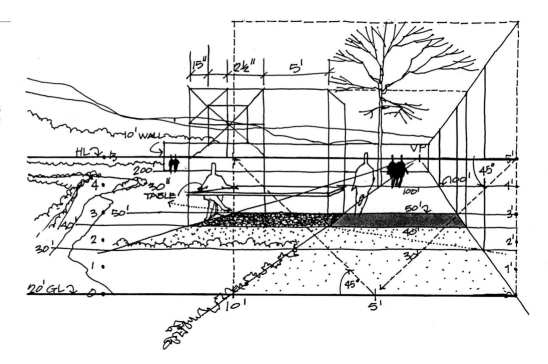

Draw horizontal lines parallel with the horizon line to create depth plane reference lines. Human figures can be drawn standing on these depth plane references and the resulting view will be what is seen by the viewer at SP.

Fig. 3-4b shows how a 45° VP may be located after depth plane reference lines have been constructed. (The 45° VP is located on HL from CV at 4 times the distance between HL and GL.) The fact that the 45 degree diagonals cross at the corners verifies that the floor has truly been divided into 10' (3m) squares. These diagonals can be used to generate other 10' (3m) squares as they cross additional 10' (3m) depth plane lines, as shown in the sketch. This principle can be applied to freehand sketching using visual judgment for establishing proportional divisions as shown in Fig. 3-5.

Freehand One-point Perspective Construction

The geometry of a one-point 5' (1.5m) eye-level perspective can be further simplified by studying the proportional relationships mentioned earlier. Fig. 3-6 illustrates the rather elegant simplicity of one-point perspective geometry, which can be reduced to two opposing overlapping 45 degree isosceles triangles, arranged so that their respective vertices touch each other's base at mid-point, forming a square inscribed by their sides. The sequence of construction is indicated in four sequential drawings. The triangles can be of any size, because the proportional relationships remain constant.

1. Begin the drawings by constructing triangle "abc" as shown.
2. Construct triangle "def" so that point "e" falls at the mid-point of line "ab". Point "c" is the VP; point "a" is the 45° VP; point "b" is the face diagonal VP;

and line "ef" indicates the 10' (3m) depth line. A horizontal line passing through the intersection of line "af" and "ec" establishes the 20' (6m) GL or the base of the PP.

3. The perspective structure can now be divided using lines "ef" and "ed" as 10' (3m) horizontal and vertical scales respectively. A construction detail may be studied in Fig. 3-6.1.

Fig. 3-6

Depth geometry of a 5' (1.5m) eye-level one-point perspective view:
A method of one-point eye-level perspective construction using the simplified geometry of two interlocking isosceles triangles. Note the location of 10' (3m) and 20' (6m) depth plane references. Points "d", "e", and "f" can be vanished back to establish 10' (3m) vertical and horizontal measurement distances. The 4-step sequence of construction are shown in greater detail in figure 3-6.1.

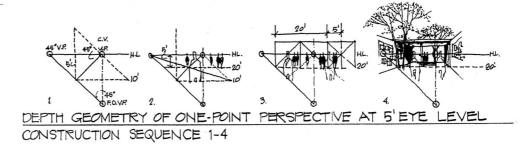

DEPTH GEOMETRY OF ONE-POINT PERSPECTIVE AT 5' EYE LEVEL
CONSTRUCTION SEQUENCE 1-4

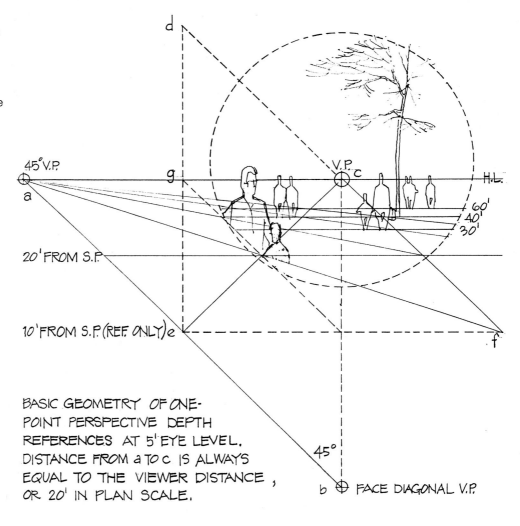

BASIC GEOMETRY OF ONE-POINT PERSPECTIVE DEPTH REFERENCES AT 5' EYE LEVEL. DISTANCE FROM a TO c IS ALWAYS EQUAL TO THE VIEWER DISTANCE, OR 20' IN PLAN SCALE.

Fig. 3-6.1

One point perspective depth geometry construction detail:

Step 1: Draw a horizon line (HL) and locate VP at the CV. Construct the two isosceles triangles as shown, with the understanding that the size of the drawing (distance from HL to GL) will be determined by 1/2 the value of the triangle leg.

Step 2: Locate the 20' (6m) GL by bisecting the distance between HL and the bottom leg of the dashed triangle, using the newly established 45° VP. These two steps have created the HL, the VP, the two 45° VPs, and the initial ground line.

Step 3: Using the distance between HL and GL to represent 5' (1.5m), the GL is divided into 10' (3m) increments, vanished back to VP, and gridded into depth planes using the 45° VP.

Step 4: Space defining elements are drawn in using the normal drawing methods outlined earlier to complete the space representation. The space is enhanced through the use of people in various parts of the drawing.

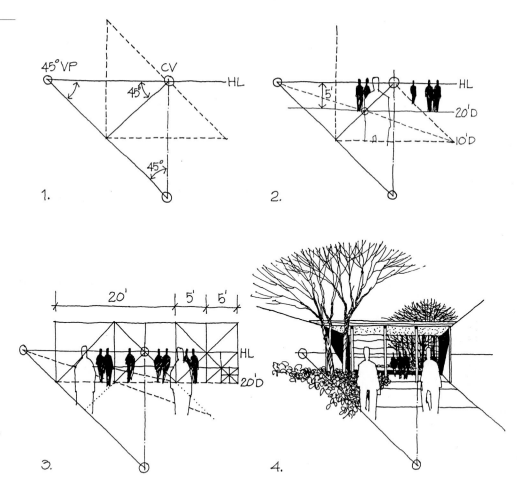

Fig. 3-7

Diagonal VPs of contiguous horizontal and vertical planes in perspective:
Application of triangle geometry to one-point perspective space frame. Cubes can be plunged below the floor plane and above the horizon line using the vertical face diagonal VP. Also, other squares can be generated by using the 45° VP.

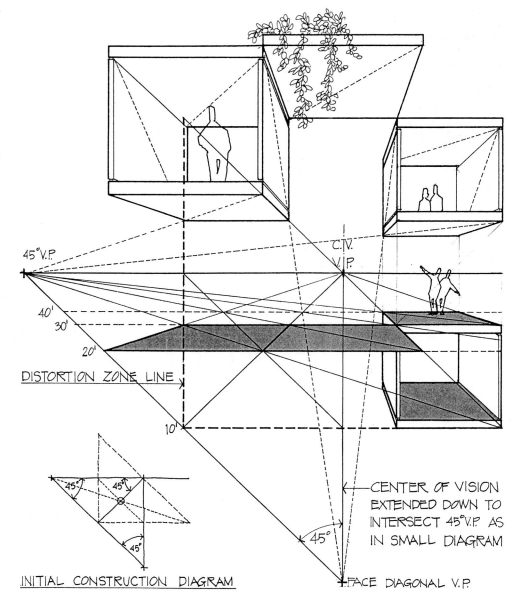

45° V.P.

C.V.
V.P.

40'
30'
20'

DISTORTION ZONE LINE

10'

45°

CENTER OF VISION EXTENDED DOWN TO INTERSECT 45° V.P. AS IN SMALL DIAGRAM

45°   45°

45°

45°

INITIAL CONSTRUCTION DIAGRAM

FACE DIAGONAL V.P.

Fig. 3-7 illustrates the application of this system for constructing a space grid directly in perspective, without reference to a plan. It also illustrates the use of face diagonals.

Fig. 3-8

One point perspective with 45° VP and depth scaling guides:
Construction of one-point perspective for free-hand sketching using depth scaling guides at sides of sketch. Depth is determined by proportional division of space between GL and HL. Initial 10' (3m) square is constructed on PP using vertical 5' (1.5m) scale vanished back to VP. An initial floor plane square is found by drawing the 40' (12m) and the 50' (15m) depth reference lines 1/2 and 2/5.

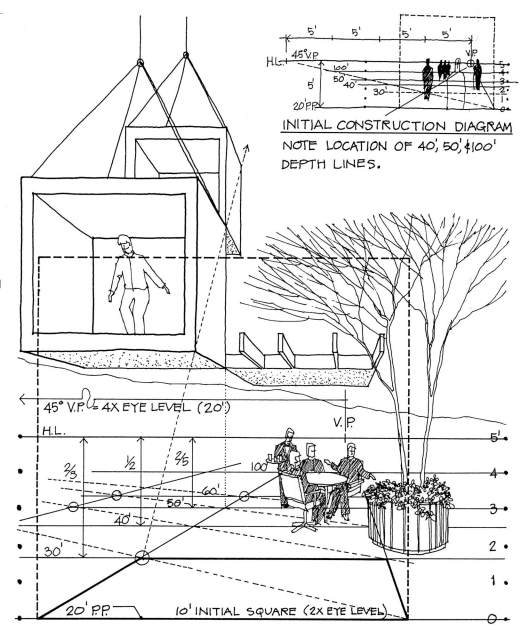

INITIAL CONSTRUCTION DIAGRAM
NOTE LOCATION OF 40', 50', & 100' DEPTH LINES.

Depth Scaling Guides

The main values of one-point landscape perspective are its ease of construction and its applicability to design process graphics. The "depth scaling guide" system of sketching is another method of sketch construction and is illustrated in Fig. 3-8. The construction diagram shows an initial HL and PP ground line drawn to any desired size, followed by an initial vertical square (in dashed line), the lower right hand corner of which has been vanished back to the 45° VP.

Fig. 3-9

Application of depth guides to pencil sketches of natural landscape scenes:
Freehand field sketches may be constructed quickly and accurately if approximate distances are known, or can be obtained from a map. Note that the people on the shore are higher than the viewer, and the person fishing is lower than the viewer.

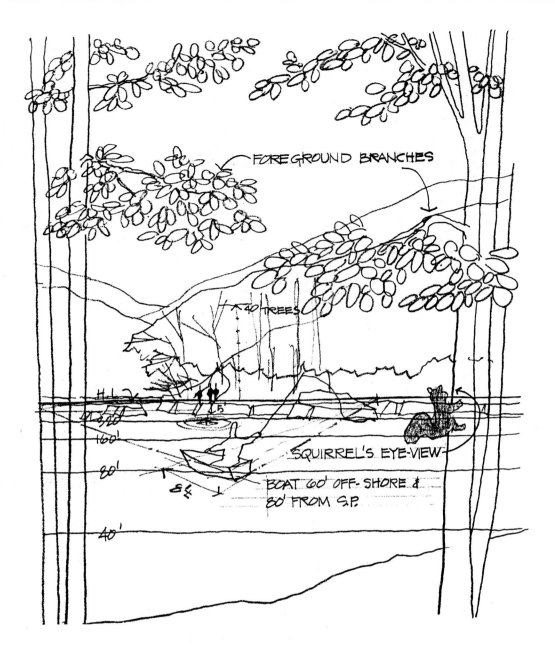

FOREGROUND BRANCHES

40' TREES

SQUIRREL'S EYE-VIEW

BOAT 60' OFF-SHORE & 80' FROM S.P.

Next, the depth plane reference lines are drawn, using as proportional guides the 5 dots to the right and left of the sketch. These "dots" represent 1' (0.25m) vertical measuring scale increments which may also be used to visually divide the HL-GL distance to determine depth plane locations. Note that the dots 3 and 4 will always equal 50' (15m) and 100' (30m) respectively. The initial horizontal square can be found by drawing the 40' (12m) and 50' (15m) depth plane reference lines, that will intersect the vanished lower corners of the initial vertical square.

Figs. 3-9 and 3-10 show how this system may be applied to field sketches where observed horizontal distances are known to be approximately correct. These two drawings show the initial layout and a quick soft pencil rendering technique. (Note strokes and tonal values.)

Fig. 3-10

Pencil overlay sketch of drawing in Fig. 3-9:
A quick rendering technique using soft pencil on a tracing overlay can convert "visual field notes" into a presentation sketch for use at a later time in the design process.

Serial Vision One-point Perspective

Serial vision sequence is an extremely important aspect of site planning in general, and urban design more specifically.

■ *The ability to "animate" a potential pedestrian sequence through a series of co-ordinated one-point perspective views, is an invaluable aid in assessing its potential visual quality.* [22]

Figs. 3-11 and 3-12 illustrate the effects of serial vision sketching, applied to a simple subject in Fig. 3-11, and a slightly more complicated subject in Fig. 3-12. In each sketch within a particular sequence, the actual eye level distance between HL and PP does not change, but the viewer position does change. So that true animation can occur, the same 5' (1.5m) value used in the 100' (30m) view must also be used for the 40' (12m) view. Changing the actual value of the 5' (1.5m) distance merely enlarges or reduces the size of the sketch. To see more detail, as with a camera, we move closer to the subject.

In serial sketches, it is good practice to use foreground figures because they create the illusion that the viewer is moving among people thereby enhancing depth illusion. Fig. 3-11 illustrates the difference between a 50' (15m) view,

Fig. 3-11

Serial perspective of a building entrance walk:
An illustration of one-point perspective applied to serial vision study of an elementary building entrance sequence. Note how the visual cones of each SP indicated in the plan inset determines the outer edges of the perspective sketches.

MAXIMUM VISUAL ACUITY: 30°

VIEWER 100' AWAY FROM BUILDING FACE

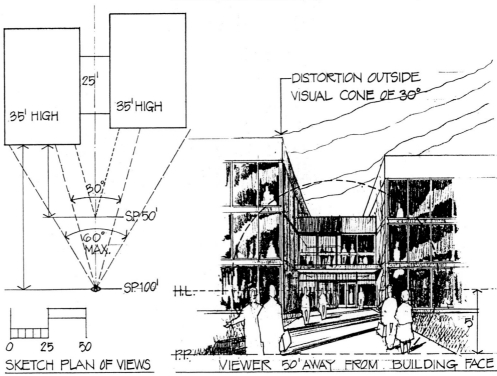

25'

35' HIGH   35' HIGH

30°

SP. 50'

60° MAX.

SP. 100'

0   25   50

SKETCH PLAN OF VIEWS

DISTORTION OUTSIDE VISUAL CONE OF 30°

H.L.

P.P.

5'

VIEWER 50' AWAY FROM BUILDING FACE

and a 100' (30m) view of the same building group and its approach walk. Notice how the plan sketch, which shows the visual cone projections, is used to determine the left and right edge of the two sketches. Fig. 3-12 demonstrates the visual power of an animated pedestrian movement toward a spatial objective. Again as in Fig. 3-11, the extreme foreground figures are used to increase the illusion of depth and to imply space with minimal use of "entourage" elements. Fig. 3-13 illustrates how a driver's eye-view might be used to generate useful serial sketches.

Fig. 3-12

Spatial animation using serial perspective:
Serial vision sequence of important pedestrian movement toward a Fine Arts Center (University of Massachusetts, Roche and Dinkaloo, Architects). Note that the 5' (1.5m) eye-level scale must remain the same. The buildings become larger because the viewer is moving closer to them.

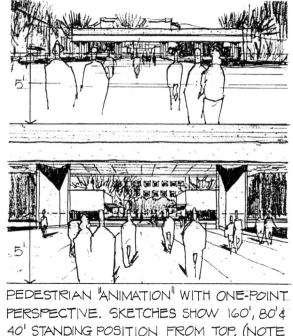

PEDESTRIAN "ANIMATION" WITH ONE-POINT PERSPECTIVE. SKETCHES SHOW 160', 80' & 40' STANDING POSITION FROM TOP. (NOTE PICTURE PLANE-HORIZON LINE DISTANCE.)

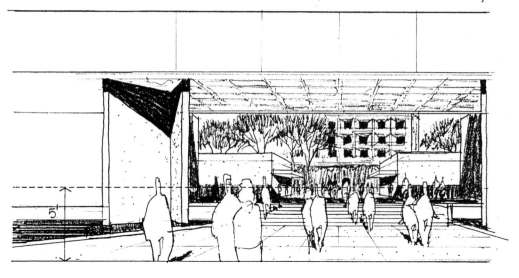

Fig. 3-13

Animating the driver's perspective:
Typical subject for a serial vision sequence: a motor parkway. Sketches could be shown at 50' (15m) to 100' (30m) intervals either on site, from photographs, or from a road plan.

Aerial Perspective Construction

One-point aerial perspective is achieved by elevating the viewer relative to the ground plane. As in eye-level perspective, the viewer's head is assumed to be erect and still, and not "tipping" downwards, which would create three-point perspective. Using the system presented in this chapter, aerial perspective becomes a simple matter of multiplying the vertical and depth scales by a proportional multiplier. Fig. 3-14 illustrates the concept of multiplying the value of established scales, without altering the apparent size of the drawing. It is important to differentiate between the scale of a sketch, which refers to the real life area represented, and the size of a sketch, which refers to size of the drawing, and not the real life content represented.

Fig. 3-14

Relationship of viewer height and distance to perceived space:
An illustration of changing the scale of a normal 5' (1.5m) eye-level drawing by multiplying all distance values by a common multiplier. In the case shown, all vertical, horizontal, and depth values have been multiplied by 5. People are reduced to 1/5 normal size, or 5 times smaller than they appear in the "normal" 5' (1.5m) eye-level view.

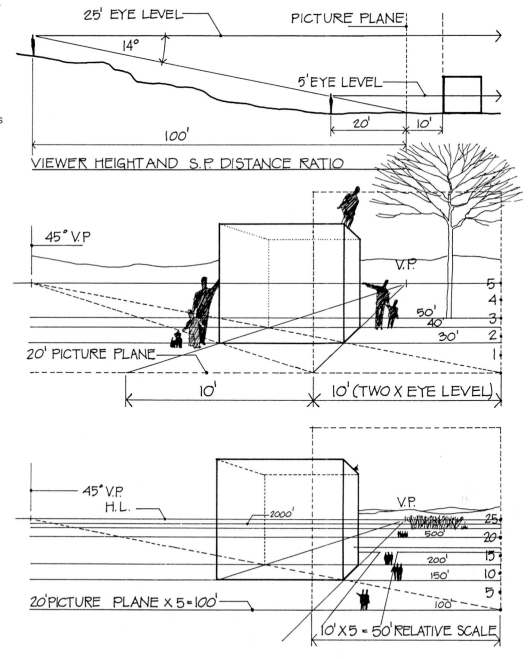

The section in Fig. 3-14 shows two individuals viewing a landscape scene. One viewer has a 25' (7.5m) eye-level and the other has a 5' (1.5m) eye-level. So that both viewers can view the same point on the ground, which is 20' (6m) away from the lower person, the higher viewer must move back far enough to allow the cone of vision to fall at the same ground line. (Note the similarity between Fig. 3-14, and previously cited Figs. 2-4 and 2-5.) The 5' (1.5m) eye-level has a 1 : 4 eye-level to picture plane distance ratio of 5' (1.5m) to 20' (6m); likewise, the 25' (7.5m) eye-level has a 1 : 4 ratio of 25' (7.5m) to 100' (15m). In other words, though the vertical eye-level and picture plane distance values change in aerial perspective, their ratio remains the same.

The two perspective sketches in Fig. 3-14 are both the same size, but their respective scales differ by a multiplier of 5. For example, 5' (1.5m) eye-level x 5 = 25' (7.5m) eye-level; 20' (6m) PP x 5 = 100' (30m) PP; 40' (12m) depth plane reference x 5 = 200' (60m); the human figures have been reduced to 1/5 their "normal" size. At any depth reference line, people are always 1/5 the distance to the horizon line. The initial cube is 50' (15m) square instead of 10' (3m) square, and the 45° VP generates 50' (15m) squares on the ground plane. It is easiest to first draw a normal 5' (1.5m) eye-level sketch to the desired size, locate the depth plane references, construct a grid on the floor plane, and then to change the scale by adding people or trees as reference guides at the scale calculated for the particular aerial view. It will simplify matters if multiples of 5 or 10 are used to establish the aerial viewing height, such as 25' (7.5m), 50' (15m), 100' (30m), 200' (60m), 250' (75m), etc.

- *Large scale landscape perspectives are valuable to both the landscape planner, as well as the landscape architect, because both are concerned with assessing the potential pattern and visual configuration of proposed land use concepts, on a specific and general scale.*

Fig. 3-15 is a photograph of the Connecticut River looking south towards Amherst, Massachusetts, at an elevation of approximately 500' (150m) above the rather flat agricultural valley floor. At this elevation, vegetation and open space patterns are clearly delineated, and large foreground trees are discernable as individual specimens. The photo shows a portion of an approximately 100 square mile (259km²) valley. Before attempting to draw large scale landscapes, it is advisable to visually experience and to document what is possible to be seen of a landscape from various viewing heights.

The aerial landscape perspective drawing shown in Fig. 3-16 represents a refinement of the basic technique presented in Fig. 3-14, and can be understood, if first analyzed as a normal 5' (1.5m) eye-level perspective in its initial construction phase. As in the previous example, the eye-level height, the picture plane distance, and the depth plane reference values have been multiplied by 100 to elevate the viewer to 500' (150m) above the floor plane, and move the viewer 2000' (600m) away from the PP ground line. An initial 1000' (300m) square is drawn on the ground plane at the picture plane reference line, or 2000' (600m) away from the viewer by using intersecting vanished

Fig. 3-15

An oblique aerial view of an agricultural valley from an elevation of approximately 500' (150m). Note the clear pattern of open spaces and the scale of trees in foreground.

Fig. 3-16

Landscape planning application of space grid enlarged 100 times: An aerial perspective view of a large scale landscape. All height and distance values of a normal 5' (1.5m) eye-level perspective have been multiplied by 100 to achieve a 500' (15m) eye-level. Note foreground scaling elements and the manner in which large areas may be mapped as indicated by the shaded zone.

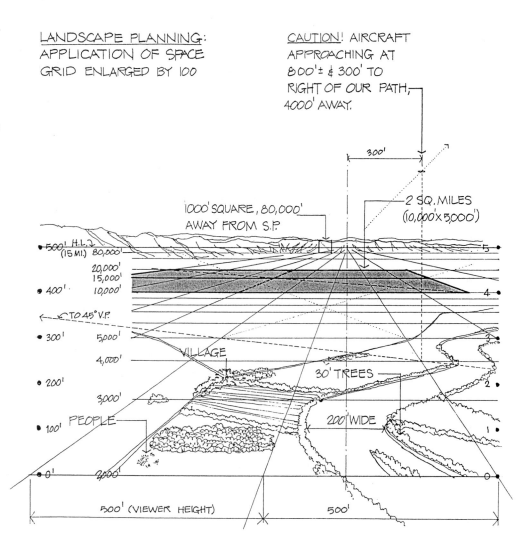

LANDSCAPE PLANNING:
APPLICATION OF SPACE
GRID ENLARGED BY 100

CAUTION! AIRCRAFT
APPROACHING AT
800'± & 300' TO
RIGHT OF OUR PATH,
4000' AWAY.

300'

2 SQ. MILES
(10,000' x 5,000')

1000' SQUARE, 80,000'
AWAY FROM S.P.

500' H.L. (15 MI.) 80,000'
20,000'
15,000'
400' 10,000'
TO 45° V.P.
300' 5,000'
4,000'
VILLAGE
200' 3,000'
30' TREES
100' PEOPLE
200' WIDE
0' 2,000'

500' (VIEWER HEIGHT)   500'

grid lines and depth reference lines. Additional floor plane squares are constructed by division and interception of 45 degree square diagonals.

The initial construction is illustrated in Fig. 3-17. It should be noted in Fig. 3-17 that any depth plane reference line drawn halfway between the HL and any other depth plane reference locates a depth reference which doubles the value of the previous depth plane. For example, the line halfway between HL and 10,000' (3000m), locates the 20,000' (6000m) depth plane, and the subsequent halving of the space remaining, locates the 40,000' (12000m) depth plane line. This "halving principle" is true for the entire system. The vertical scale and depth measurement "dots" are labeled 0-5' (0-1.5m) on the right hand side of the drawing, and are "converted" to 0-500' (0-150m) on the left side of the drawing (see Fig. 3-8 for review of technique).

The space grid is given cultural meaning by adding a minimal number of human scaling elements, such as the airplane, the village center, the cultivated field, the 30' (9m) trees, and the group of people shown in the foreground who are standing in a field just over 2000' (600m) away from the viewer and who are well within the threshold of perception (recall from Chapter 2 that we should be able to see people as far away as 4000' (120m)).

Fig. 3-17

Initial construction of a 1000' (300m) square for a one-point aerial perspective.
Diagram of initial construction technique used to achieve a landscape space grid. Initial 1000' square is used to generate others by sub-division with diagonals and depth plane reference lines. Note the use of scaling dots at the left and right sides, as earlier shown in Fig. 3-8.

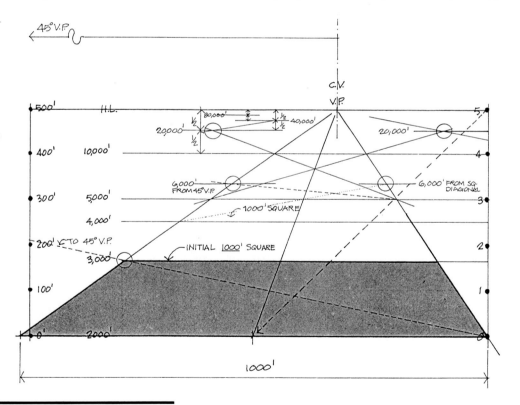

Child's Eye-View Perspective Construction

A "child's eye-view" perspective is very valuable for illustrating playground design, child-centered designs, or for adding more drama to a perspective view. The procedure is the same one used for normal 5' (1.5m) eye-level perspective, but the eye-level and picture plane distance, and the depth plane references are halved in value, and results in the scale shown in Fig. 3-18. Where the previously illustrated aerial view expands the spatial values and distances, the child's eye-view reduces them. Fig. 3-18 is constructed by laying out an initial 5' (1.5m) ground plane square, using the ground line (GL) to establish its front or leading edge. The shaded area represents a square that would have a 10' (3m) side if drawn to normal scale. All adults and objects taller than 2.5' (0.75m) need to be vertically scaled using multiples of the ground to HL distance; in other words, all points on the ground at any depth are 2.5' (0.75m) below the horizon line (HL).

The one-point perspective is the most versatile and widely-used perspective view for representing landscape space because it is simple to draw, and because the predominantly "biomorphic" forms of landscape open space very rarely require a specific oblique view with reference to a structural grid. However, work involving architecture or interior court spaces often requires oblique views, and these techniques are presented in the chapters which follow.

Fig. 3-18

A 2.5' (0.75m) child's eye-level perspective view: A child's eye-view achieved by reducing all dimensional and depth values by 1/2. Note that the picture plane distance is now 10' (3m) instead of 20' (6m). A simple cross-section will explain why. Adult eye level is above the horizon line and trees seem to "tower" over spaces (see Fig. 3-1).

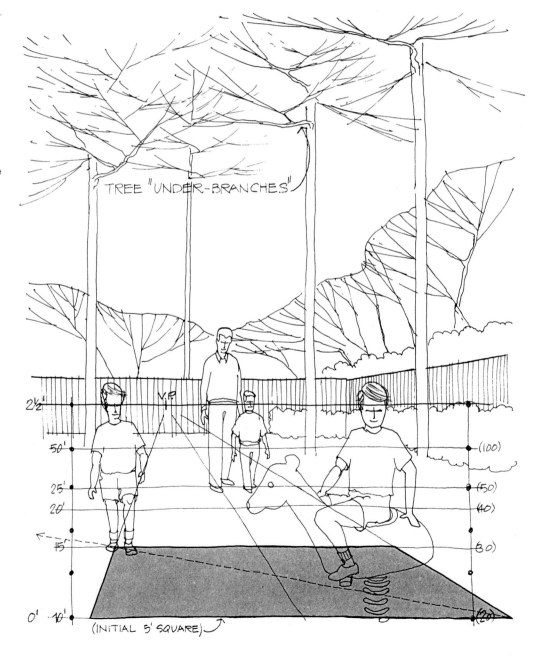

TREE "UNDER-BRANCHES"

V.P

2½"

50'   (100)
25'   (50)
20'   (40)
15'   (30)
0' 10'   (20)

(INITIAL 5' SQUARE)

4

Two-Point Perspective

Plan Projection Construction Methods: 30/60 Degree, and 20/70 Degree

The theoretical principles of depth and perspective illusion presented in Chapters 2 and 3 apply also to the two-point perspective view. The purpose of Chapter 4 is to illustrate the traditional, or "classic" method of constructing two-point perspective views, with the objectives of: (1) simplifying the method and converting it to the "direct drawing" method shown in Chapter 3; and (2) illustrating design drawing applications.

Although the construction is a bit more complicated, the two-point view assumes that the viewer is standing at a specific point, with head erect and looking toward the horizon with a fixed gaze. In typical architectural perspective, the viewer stands at an oblique angle to the building being viewed. In this orientation, there are no building lines parallel to the viewer's center line of vision and consequently no building or grid lines converge on the CV, as occurs in one-point perspective. Instead, the oblique orientation results in two vanishing points, at which all perpendicular building or grid lines converge on the horizon line, as illustrated in Fig. 4-1.

■ *In landscape perspective, the two-point view is used when an important rectangular ground pattern is being illustrated, or when important buildings are in the foreground and require considerable detail rendition.*

Interior views of garden courtyards often require an oblique view to capture an important feature. In such cases, a slightly oblique view, such as the 20/70 degree view is used to add interest, but avoid distortion. The 30/60

Fig. 4-1

Comparison of plan layout and resulting perspective views for 30/60 and 20/70 degree viewer orientation: An illustration of two common oblique angles used for two-point perspective. Note that as geometric figures approach the peripheral vision area (outside of the cone of vision), they become elongated and distorted. Cubes drawn within the 30 degree cone appear to be "believable" cubes (after Lockard).

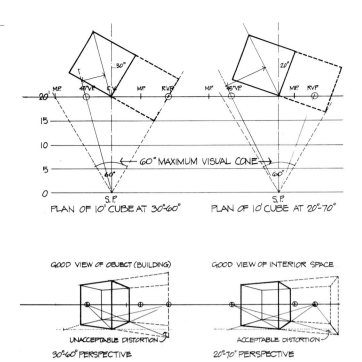

degree view, is useful when drawing objects with facades, such as buildings, or when more drama is required to illustrate a floor or wall pattern containing strong diagonal lines, or visual lines of force.

Fig. 4-1 illustrates in abbreviated fashion, the plan and perspective relationship of "classically" constructed two-point perspective, showing 30/60 and 20/70 degree views of a 10' (3m) cube with a dashed line extension which pierces the picture plane (PP). From the plan view, it can be observed that the cube extension is more distorted in the 30/60 degree view than is the case in the 20/70 degree view, thus illustrating the greater interior view suitability of the 20/70 degree perspective. This "unacceptable distortion" occurs because the drawing is requiring the eye and the brain to rationalize a view which if seen in a real setting, would require the viewer to "back up" in order to truly encompass it. However, if drawn very lightly as a "vignette," the dashed line in the 20/70 degree view could approximate the peripheral nature of real scale vision and could be used to good advantage. Note that the "acceptable distortion" indicated in the 20/70 degree perspective is well over 15' (4.5m) from the viewer at SP.

If compared to Fig. 3-3 it can be seen that the plan views in both figures have similar features; the differences are found in the 45° VP location, the picture plane and cube relationship, and absence of a true square in perspective. However, in each instance, the viewer is standing 20' from the picture plane, which is located on the ground by the 14 degree angle of the vertical cone of vision (see Fig. 3-1). The depth plane reference lines also have a similar proportional relationship with viewer height and horizon line and ground line distance, as will be presented later. The absence of a "true" square, which can be constructed by visual judgment, requires special construction techniques to achieve an initial square and cube.

In two-point perspective, vertical cube walls facing the viewer are trapezoids, not true squares. Therefore, measurements on the X axis are proportional derivations, not direct multiples of the vertical scale, as is the case in one-point perspective. This fact requires a method of transferring true scale distances to proportionally diminished ones on the X and Z axis. It is called, "the measuring point projection method."

Measuring Point Projection Method

Fig. 4-2 illustrates the "classic" measuring point projection method for constructing a 30/60 degree two-point perspective view. The steps for construction are summarized as follows:

Step 1: A plan view of a 10' (3m) cube is drawn with its front corner touching the picture plane, and its sides at a 30/60 degree angle in relation to the picture plane, and therefore the viewer.

Step 2: The SP is located 20' (6m) away from the picture plane as shown. From the SP, lines parallel to the facing sides of the cube are projected until they intersect with an extension of the picture plane to the left and to the right. These intersections locate the Left Vanishing Point (LVP) and the Right Vanishing Point (RVP).

Step 3: Arcs (dashed lines) drawn from the SP and centered on the respective vanishing points are swung to intercept the picture plane line, thus locating the two measuring points (MP).

Step 4: A line parallel to the cube diagonal is drawn from the SP to the picture plane, and locates the 45° VP on the PP.

Step 5: A horizon line is drawn below the plan, and the newly constructed points (LVP, RVP, MP, CV, and 45° VP) are projected down to intercept it, as shown in Fig. 3-2 by the fine dotted lines.

Step 6: The leading cube corner is drawn at the CV point at the same scale used to draw the plan. Since the perspective view is to have a 5' (1.5m) eye level, the base corner of the cube can be scaled at 5' (1.5m) below the horizon line and the top corner can be located in similar fashion to establish the 10' (3m) leading edge (this is the only part of the drawing that is drawn to true scale because it is "touching" the picture plane).

Step 7: The top and bottom of this leading edge are vanished to the left and right vanishing points (LVP and RVP) which establish the top and bottom cube face edges. To find the remaining cube edges, the measuring points are employed.

Fig. 4-2

Comparison of standard and modified measuring point perspective construction of a 30/60 degree view:

Traditional method of 30/60 degree two-point perspective construction using measuring points (MP) and corner projections from SP, results in the top plan and perspective drawing. The horizon line distribution ratio of LVP, MP, CV, MP, RVP is shown as a fixed proportional relationship for all 30/60 degree views using a 20' (6m) SP-PP distance.

The modified distribution of these points is illustrated in the lower drawing, which fixes them at even fractions between LVP and RVP. Note the "slight discrepancy" between the constructed version above and the modified version of even ratios below (after Walters and Bromham).

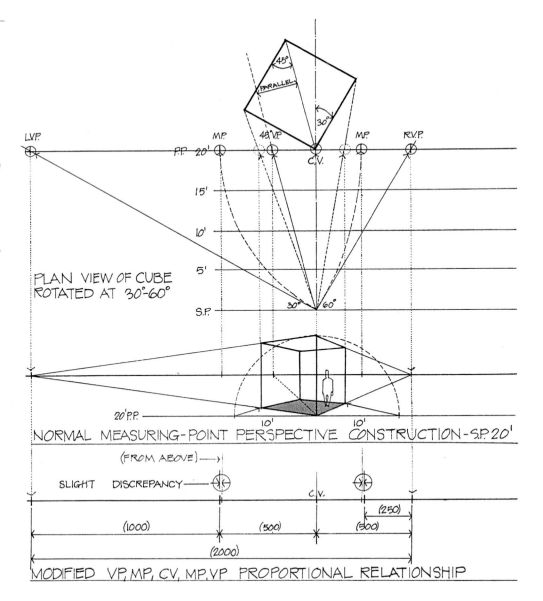

PLAN VIEW OF CUBE ROTATED AT 30°-60°

NORMAL MEASURING-POINT PERSPECTIVE CONSTRUCTION-S.P. 20'

MODIFIED VP, MP, CV, MP, VP PROPORTIONAL RELATIONSHIP

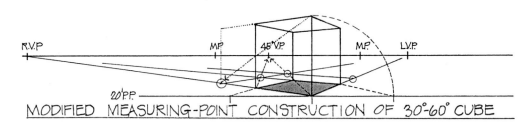

MODIFIED MEASURING-POINT CONSTRUCTION OF 30°-60° CUBE

Step 8: Transfer the 10' (3m) vertical leading edge dimension of the cube, down to the picture plane ground line (GL) by swinging an arc, or using a 45° triangle to locate two points equi-distant from the leading edge on the picture plane GL. These points are used in the next step employing the measuring points (MP).

Step 9: The ground line points represent the true dimension of the corresponding cube edges and are vanished to the opposing measuring points, intercepting the vanished cube base edges, and locating the back vertical cube edges (this is the main function of the measuring points). These back edges can be alternately located by bringing down projected cube edges indicated by dotted lines. If this alternative method of locating the other two visible cube edges is used, a line from SP to each cube corner must be drawn, and their intersections at the PP are projected down as indicated by the fine dotted lines. It is possible to create more cubes or ground plane squares by repeating the measuring point procedure after laying out additional 10' (3m) increments on the picture plane (PP) line.

Step 10: The remaining lines of the cube may be drawn, to show its interior, or exterior surfaces.

Step 11: The ground plane surface may be subdivided further by using the 45° VP to vanish all 10' (3m) square diagonals drawn from the corners of previously constructed cubes or ground plane squares. This procedure is illustrated in the bottom construction of Fig. 4-2.

Modified Measuring Point Method

The measuring point construction method shown in Fig. 4-2 illustrates that for every 30/60 degree, 5' (1.5m) eye-level perspective view, which is being seen from a 20' (6m) SP, there is a predictable proportional distribution of the LVP, MPs, 45° VP, CV, and RVP along the horizon line (HL). This unique distribution is almost divisible by even fractions as shown in the third drawing of Fig. 4-2. Indeed, if "even fractions" are superimposed upon the HL, only slight discrepancies occur at the MP locations, which for all practical purposes can be ignored without any undue harm to the construction process and the visual outcome.[23] This modification is a key to converting the plan projection method into the direct drawing system.

Fig. 4-3 graphically summarizes the steps in constructing a 30/60 degree cube space frame using the modified version of the measuring point system.

Step 1: Lay out a horizon line to a desired length and mark the LVP and RVP. Bisect the line to establish MP_1, and bisect the remaining distance to locate CV (the CV point will be the location of the initial cube edge). Bisect the distance between CV and RVP to find MP_2 (These even fraction values are derived form the drawing in Fig. 4-2). To establish the 5' (1.5m) eye-level scale, the distance between CV and RVP must be divided into four parts and subsequently, the first part (commencing at CV) must be subdivided into five units as shown. The distance between CV and RVP represents the 20' (6m) "viewer distance" which has been proportionally compressed by 60 degrees (see previous plan layout in Fig. 4-2). Therefore, using a 60 degree angle, and counting over five units from CV, draw a line to intersect a vertical extension of CV to find point O, which will establish the picture plane location.[24]

Step 2: Transfer the 5' (1.5m) eye-level distance to a line extending above the horizon line to establish the 10' (3m) front cube corner and vanish the top and bottom of the corner to LVP and RVP. Transfer by means of a 45 degree angle or a compass arc, the 10' (3m) value down to the picture plane (or measuring line). Connect these dimension points with opposing MP_1 and MP_2, to intercept vanished cube base edges.

Fig. 4-3

Construction sequence of 30/60 degree two-point perspective using modified measuring point system and direct drawing vertical height derivation (see step one):

(1) Layout HL and locate RVP and LVP. Derive GL height using triangular extrapolation of CV-RVP distance as shown. Construct initial cube and space grid as shown in steps 2-4 using normal drawing techniques.

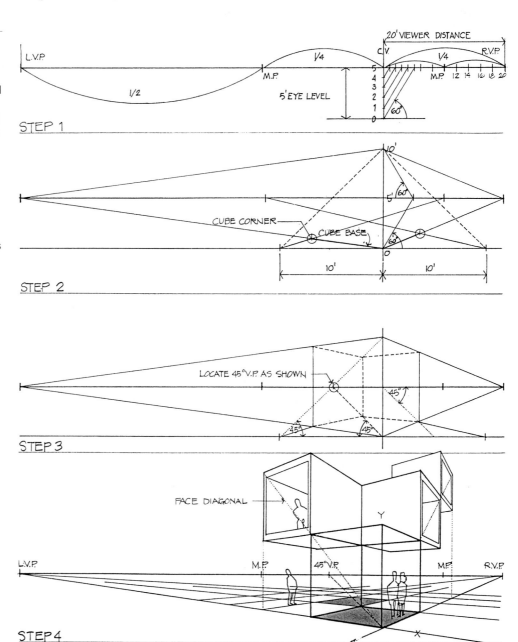

Fig. 4-4

Enlarged construction detail of 30/60 degree cube perspective using HL divisions without reference to a plan:
Note that a pre-established vertical scale at CV can determine the LVP and RVP spacing, or the vertical scale at CV can be derived from a pre-determined LVP and RVP distance using the proportional divisions shown. The dotted lines are drawn with a 30/60 degree triangle (after Doblin).

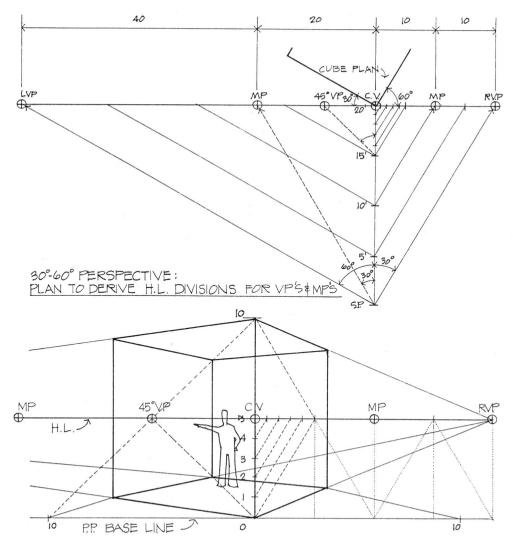

30°-60° PERSPECTIVE:
PLAN TO DERIVE H.L. DIVISIONS FOR VP'S & MP'S

DETERMINE VERTICAL SCALE FROM HORIZON LINE (H.L.) DIVISIONS, OR FIND H.L. DIVISIONS FROM PRE-DETERMINED VERTICAL SCALE

Step 3: Draw a vertical line at each intersection to complete the cube faces. Vanish rear cube edges to establish the initial floor plane square, and extend the diagonal to the horizon line to establish the 45° VP.

Step 4: Replicate other floor plane squares and cube faces by using 45° VP and face diagonals. (See Fig. 4-4 for further drawings.)

Direct Drawing Method

The method outlined in Fig. 4-3 can be simplified one step further. Fig. 4-4 illustrates a plan derivation of the critical perspective points on the horizon line (LVP, MP$_1$, 45° VP, CV, MP$_2$, RVP). The perspective sketch shown, however, needs no plan construction and can be drawn directly in the perspective view shown.

First establish a horizon line and a CV intersection. By earlier demonstration it was established that the CV in 30/60 degree perspective is always equidistant from the RVP and MP. It was also shown that the vertical scale is always equal to 1/4 of the distance between CV and RVP, proportionally enlarged by a 60 degree angle (see plan above for proof). It is therefore possible to generate the entire drawing by working "backwards" from a pre-determined vertical scale, or to derive a vertical scale from a pre-determined horizon line length.

The plan layout for Fig. 4-4 illustrates how the true plan scale is proportionally transferred to the picture plane (PP), and then subsequently to the horizon line (HL). Note the CV-RVP distance is divided into four units, with each unit representing 5' (1.5m), for a total of 20' (6m). The perspective sketch below the plan is constructed using the "direct drawing" method without the use of a plan projection. This method allows for quick freehand sketches which are useful for design analysis and development drawings.
Figs. 4-6 through 4-8 are examples of direct drawing study sketches which were drawn without reference to a plan construction. In other words, they were drawn solely to visualize "space," and not to verify plan layout.

■ *A danger found in direct drawing methods which must be avoided is attempting to extend the drawing too far out of the 30 degree cone of high visual acuity.*

Because their is no plan projection, the actual cone limits are not plotted and "projected down" to the sketch. However, the visual window is plottable upon the picture plane. Fig. 4-5 illustrates the visual criteria by which unacceptable

Fig. 4-5

Critical distortion areas in 30/60 degree perspective:
An example of visual distortion outside of the 30 degree cone of vision at close range. It is best to avoid these exaggerated edges. Cubes within cone appear to have visually believable proportions. Lines leading into the distortion zones should be gradually faded, if shown at all.

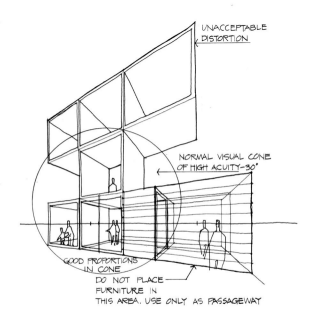

Fig. 4-6

**Construction and scaling
of a landscape from a grid:**
A direct application of a
perspective cube space to
landscape perspective
drawing. Diagram below
shows construction detail.
Vast initial planes are
humanized by locating critical
depth perception thresholds
discussed in Chapter 2.

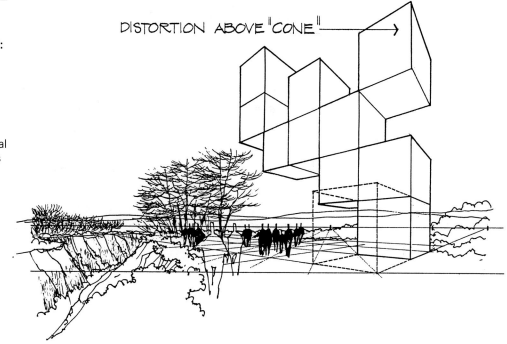

DISTORTION ABOVE "CONE"

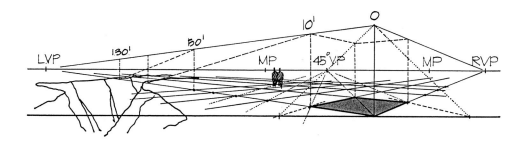

distortion may be judged. As mentioned earlier, distortion around the edge
of the visual cone may be softened if drawn as a vignette, using lighter lines
and tones.

Cube Space Grids

The cube space grids generated by this method of construction allow the
accurate plotting of landscape space for both eye-level views as shown in
Fig. 4-6, or for aerial views illustrated by Fig. 4-7. In both sketches the drawing was constructed directly into perspective, without the aid of a plan view.
Fig. 4-6 demonstrates how a landscape setting may be constructed using

Fig. 4-7

An aerial view of landscape from initial 30/ 60 degree, 100' (30m) cube space:

Values of a normal 10' (3m) cube have been enlarged by a factor of 10. Human figures have correspondingly been reduced to 1/10 "normal" size. The site boundary shows a 4 acre (1.6ha) area. Note method of construction recapitulates the method shown in Fig. 4-4.

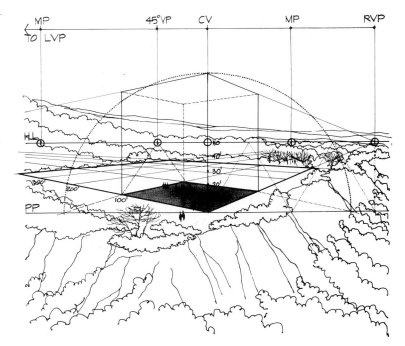

minimal information to convey the sense of a "human scaled" landscape composition, while also illustrating how easy it is to derive critical distances to ensure that the viewer is not being asked to see what would not normally be discernable (See Chapter 1).

With this cube space grid system, it is possible to accurately plot specific acreage, and to plot boundaries; Fig. 4-7 for example, shows a four-acre (1.6ha) square, superimposed on a specific site. The aerial view is derived from the basic 5' (1.5m) eye-level view, but the visual scale is altered by multiplying height and depth values in a method similar to the one previously illustrated in Figs. 3-14 and 3-16 in Chapter 3. The most effective way to understand scale changes in a perspective view is to construct an initial 10' (3m) cube space, and then to draw scale figures which have been "reduced" in size by the amount of enlargement. The people in Fig. 4-7 for example, are 1/10 their normal size, thus making the cube and ground plane squares appear to be 10 times larger; the 10' (3m) cube is now 100' (30m) high and the depth distances are similarly enlarged; the 5' (1.5m) viewer eye-level is now 50' (15m); the ground line (GL) of the picture plane is located 200' (60m) away from SP (50' (15m) x 4 = 200' (60m) due to the 1 : 4 ratio of viewer height to SP-GL distance (see Fig. 3-1, Chapter 3).

Two-Point Depth Reference Ground Plane Lines

As stated earlier, the 30/60 degree perspective view is very appropriate for showing strong diagonal spatial relationships. Fig. 4-8 represents an example of such an application. The drawing illustrates, using fine dotted lines, how the 45° VP may be employed to generate both ceiling and floorplane grid divisions from an initial cube and square. In this instance, the initial cube has been removed, and all that remains is the cube's leading edge, which is indicated by a dashed line commencing at "O". The "X" and "Y" axis converge on the LVP and RVP respectively.

As in the case of one-point perspective, depth reference lines can be determined by both the 45° VP method shown in the example, and the proportional division of the ground plane between the HL and the 20' (6m) ground line. In two-point perspective, the X axis converges onto the HL, therefore the 40' (12m) depth reference line must also converge onto the HL; but because it is further away from the viewer than the 20' (6m) line, it converges at a slower rate (more shallow angle). It can be observed in Fig. 4-8, that as the circled 40' (12m) depth reference line is traced from right to left, it is always half way between HL and the 20' (6m) depth reference line (note that in one-point perspective, the X axis is always parallel with the HL). Similarly, the same proportional convergence can be observed for the 30' (9m), 50' (15m), and 60' (18m) depth reference lines.

In other words, any even distance may be plotted directly onto the perspective floor plane using the proportional division system outlined in Chapter 2, without reference to a plan, or a pre-established grid. The direct drawing system can be refined and simplified even further, as illustrated in Figs. 4-9 through 4-11.

Fig. 4-8

Space grid from initial 10' (3m) cube using 45° VP:
An application of 30/60 degree cube space grid for interior garden courtyard view. Note that 40' (12m) depth plane reference is consistently half way between 20' (6m) X axis ground line and the horizon line; 30' (9m) is 1/3 the distance. The grid has been generated by using the initial square, and the 45° VP. Note the foreground, midground, and background triad placement of scale figures to create a feeling of human interaction and potential.

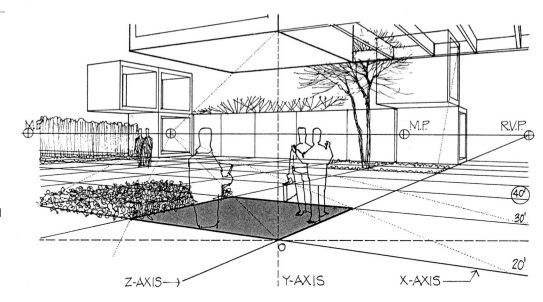

Vanishing Guideline Sketch Frame Perspective Method

Another method of perspective construction is through the use of vanishing guidelines, the construction of which is shown sequentially in Figs. 4-9, 4-10, and 4-11. This method eliminates the need for a distant vanishing point which usually requires a large drawing board for a perspective of any consequence. Fig. 4-9 shows the guidelines derived geometrically from a cube in perspective. The initial cube face has been divided into 1' (0.25m) increments and the division dots have been joined by line extensions. These lines converge onto the LVP and therefore serve as "guides" for all X axis lines, whether on the ground or on the face of vertical surfaces. The perspective sketch is drawn using a straight edge for both X and Y axis lines.

The sequence shown in Figs. 4-10 and 4-11 are based upon the previously discussed construction system. Drawing 1 in Fig. 4-10 illustrates the normal initial steps of drawing HL, establishing a vertical 5' (1.5m) scale, and then locating 45° VP, MP$_2$, RVP, and a new line called RVL (Right Vanishing Line). Drawing 2. of Fig. 4-10 shows the extension and proportional division of RVL. Essentially a value of two units from LVL are added to the top and bottom of RVL. RVL is then proportionally divided into 10 equal parts - 5 above the HL and 5 below HL. Drawing 1. of Fig. 4-11 shows LVL and RVL divisions connected by "vanishing guidelines," which converge at a distant VP (LVP). The cube is constructed in the manner shown, using MP$_2$, 45° VP, and face diagonal methods. By previous definition, the picture plane line is 20' (6m) away from the viewer. Also, note that by construction and by visual judgment, the 40' (12m) depth reference is located at half the distance between HL and the 20' (6m) depth line at any point along its length. Drawing 2. in Fig. 4-11 illustrates how a freehand sketch may be drawn within the vanishing line frame without loss of basic proportional accuracy. Lines vanishing to the left are drawn with a transparent straight edge, roughly parallel to the nearest vanishing line.

Fig. 4-9

Derivation of vanishing guideline frame from 10' (3m) cube:
An illustration of geometrical derivation of vanishing guidelines for 30/60 degree perspective.

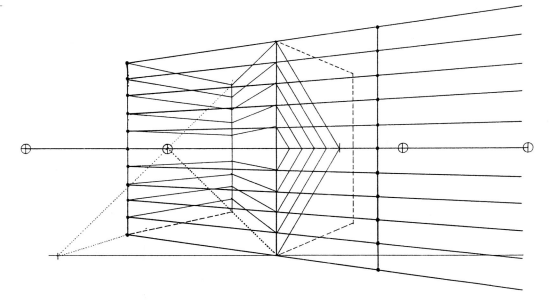

Fig. 4-10

Sequential construction of vanishing guidelines for 30/60 degree perspective:

Step 1: Layout 45° VP, CV, MP$_2$, and RVP in the usual manner.

Step 2: Divide an extension of the CV line into ten 1' (0.30m) units. This line is now called the "Left Vanishing Line" (LVL).

Step 3: Locate and construct "Right Vanishing Line" (RVL) as shown and increase in length by four units measured from the LVL.

Step 4: Re-divide the entire RVL into 10 larger units as shown. Lines connecting the measuring dots on both lines will converge toward the HL. Fig. 4-11 illustrates the completion of the construction.

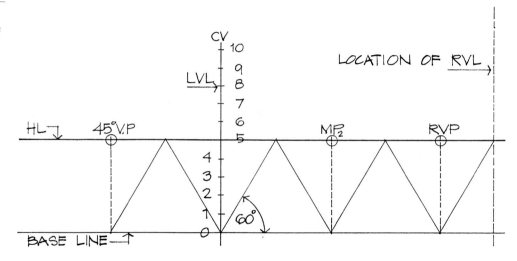

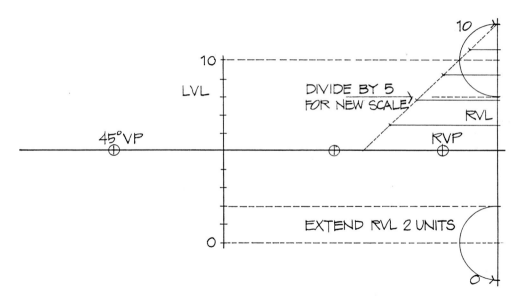

Fig. 4-11

Construction of 30/60 degree vanishing guidelines and sketch application example:

The final construction step shows lines connecting the vanishing dots located on LVL and RVL and construction of the initial cube. The drawing below represents an example using the vanishing guideline sketch frame. Note depth plane references are similar to the one-point system discussed in Chapter 3; 40' (12m) is always half of the distance between HL and the vanishing 20' (6m) X axis depth line.

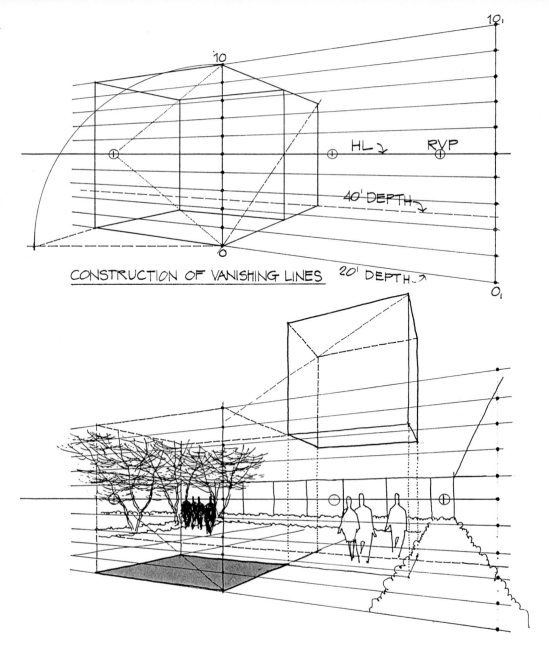

CONSTRUCTION OF VANISHING LINES

45/45 Degree Perspective Construction

Using the previously presented principles, it is possible to derive a number of proportional divisions of the HL to accommodate many different viewing angles. However, such an array of systems is not very useful for general work. It is useful, however, to examine two additional two-point perspective systems.

Fig. 4-12 illustrates the derivation of a two-point 45/45 degree perspective from a symmetrical 5' (1.5m) eye-level one-point perspective. In the one-point perspective, the two 45° VPs become the LVP and the RVP of the two-point perspective below; and the VP of the one-point perspective becomes the

45° VP in the two-point perspective. The new square grid can be generated by inscribing the initial one-point square, as shown, or by inscribing the new square within the initial one-point square. In either case, the horizontal diagonal of the new 45 degree square is equal to √2 (1.414), assuming the side of the square is equal to 1.0.[25] To find a new vertical height, the new square corners are projected forward from MP$_1$ and MP$_2$ to the new picture plane.

The example shown is more difficult than inscribing the new square within the initial one-point square, but the method in Fig. 4-12 has the effect of enlarging the sketch. The 45/45 degree perspective view is one not often used professionally, and is offered here more to demonstrate how the drawing system may be manipulated, rather than to suggest its widespread application.

Fig. 4-12

Generation of a 45/45 degree two-point perspective from a one-point 10' (3m) cube:
This method of converting symmetrical one-point perspective into 45/45 degree two-point perspective by construction is not commonly applied in professional drawing, but its principles are worth studying for deeper understanding of the descriptive geometry involved.

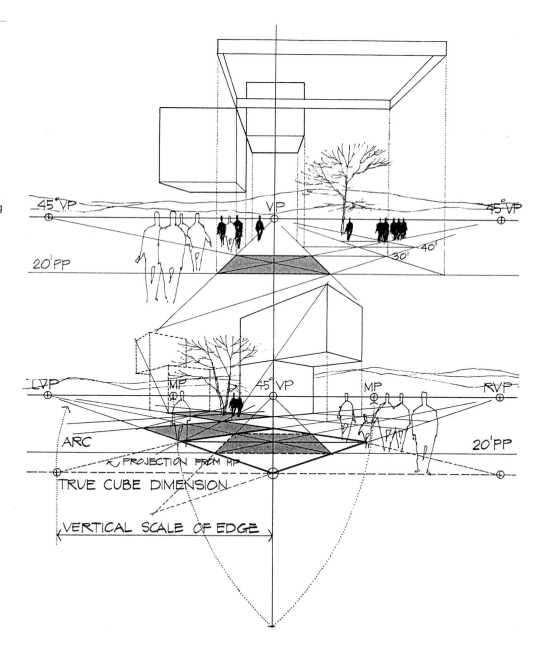

20/70 Degree Perspective Construction

Fig. 4-13 illustrates the traditional plan projection construction method for 20/70 degree two-point perspective, as well as the horizon line proportional sub-division method outlined for 30/60 degree two-point perspective earlier in this chapter (see Fig. 4-3). The horizon line subdivisions have been derived from the initial plan construction and are illustrated in the lower drawing as LVP, 40, 40, 40, MP_1, 40, CV, 10, MP_2, 10, and RVP. Although not shown for reasons of clarity, the 45° VP is located by projecting a line from the standing position (SP) to the picture plane (PP), at an angle parallel to the plan square diagonal (See Fig. 4-1). The point of intersection is then projected down to the horizon line (HL) to locate the 45° VP shown in the lower sketch of Fig. 4-13. For all practical purposes, it can be observed that the distance between CV and the 45° VP is almost equal to the initial cube corner length, which touches and rests upon the PP.

Fig. 4-13

20/70 degree space grid from proportional horizon line divisions:
The plan projection method yields a fixed proportion for LVP, MPs(1), 45° VP, CV, MP_2, and RVP distances. Lower drawing shows direct drawing method using proportions shown and constructed without a plan projection. Note in lower perspective that the 40' (12m) depth line, or the rear of the second depth square bisects the CV line between HL and GL, thus confirming the validity of the depth proportioning system established in Chapter 3 (see Fig. 3-3).

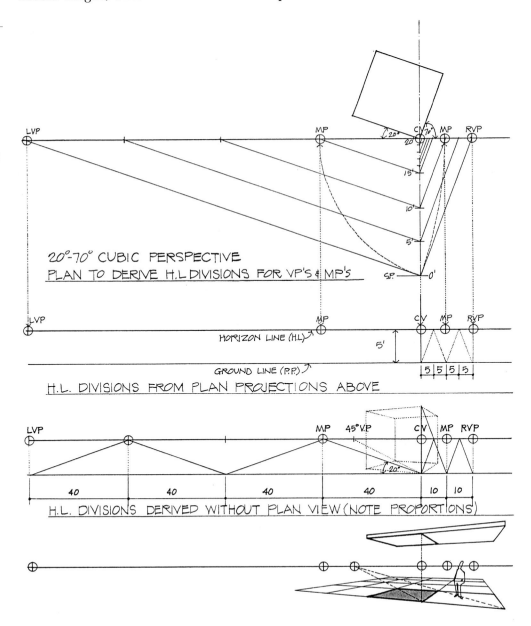

Once the LVP, MP_1, 45° VP, CV, MP_2, and RVP are located on the horizon line, the drawing may be constructed in the normal sketch frame fashion (see Fig. 4-14 for a detailed description of the layout procedure). These proportions reflect the 20/70 degree plan projections from points along the centerline of vision (CV), as they intercept the picture plane line. In other words, the LVP to CV distance on the horizon line is determined by the 20' (6m) viewer distance and the tangent function of 60° and the CV to RVP distance is derived from the tangent function of 20°.

■ *As is the case with any two-point perspective drawing using a fixed 20' (6m) SP, the distances between the CV and the respective vanishing points will always be proportional expansions or compressions of the 20' (6m) plan scale SP to PP distance.*

Consequently, the 20/70 degree triangle can be used as a proportional scale, with each leg equal to the equivalent of 5' (1.5m). The 20/70 degree perspective view is especially useful for interior courtyard views because of its shallow angle and "natural" sight lines.

Fig. 4-14 illustrates the steps used to construct a 20/70 degree sketch frame, again using techniques similar to those outlined in Figs. 4-10 and 4-11.

Step 1. (See Drawing A) Draw a horizon line, and using a desired scale to represent 5' (1.5m), draw a "base line" below it as shown. Locate the CV and draw a vertical line, scaled to represent 10' (3m). Using a 20/70 degree triangle, locate the MP_2, RVP, RVL, MP_1, and 45° VP on the horizon line (HL).

Step 2. (See Drawing B) Re-scale the RVL by dividing it into 10 larger parts using the construction method illustrated. Scale the CV line to represent 10 equal parts, based on the initial measured scale in Step 1. Connect the corresponding division values to create the vanishing guidelines as demonstrated for points "1" and "9" (See Drawing C for finished effect). Replicate

Fig. 4-14

Construction of 20/70 degree vanishing guideline sketch frame:

Drawings A, B, and C show the step-by-step procedure for constructing a vanishing guideline sketch frame which accurately locates depth planes by division. Drawing C shows people located 20' (6m) to 40' (12m) from the viewer. The shaded cube is directly behind the initial cube, and 100' (30m) away from the viewer.

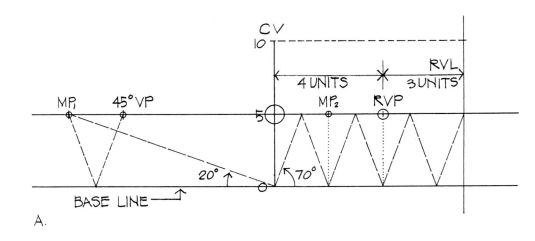

A.

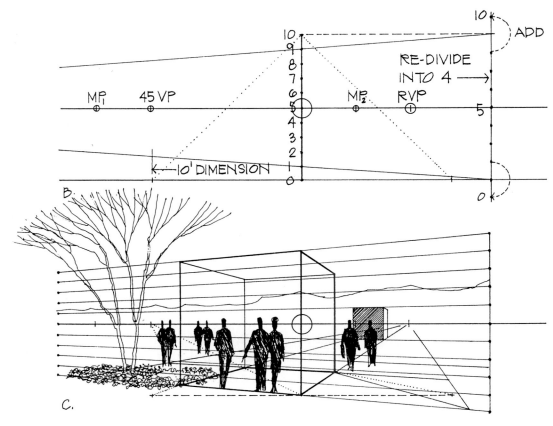

B.

C.

the length of the line at CV to the right and to the left along the base line using a 45° triangle, or a compass arc. These distances will be vanished back to the measuring points (MPs) to establish the initial cube base depth.

Step 3. (See Drawing C) Draw the initial cube using the MPs, the 45° VP, the RVP, and the vanishing guidelines, and subdivide the floor plane to establish other depth planes, or to locate objects, such as the distant shaded 10' (3m) cube, which is located 100' (30m) behind the initial cube. The figures are 20' (6m) to 40' (12m) away from the viewer (see ground plane divisions). Fig. 4-15 illustrates a large scale landscape application of the 20/70 degree sketch frame constructed in the previous figure.

Fig. 4-15

Large scale landscape application of 20/70 degree vanishing guideline sketch frame:
The sketch shows the use of the 45° VP for creating more scaling grid lines. Note that the numbered dots can also be used to calculate the depth lines; the line connecting "3" represents a 50' (15m) depth because it is 2/5 of the distance between HL and GL, and the line connecting "2.5" represents a 40' (12m) depth because it bisects the HL to GL distance (see Figure 3-3).

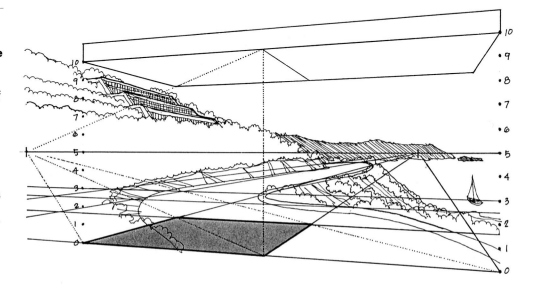

Fig. 4-16 shows a more elaborate sketch using a 20/70 degree sketch frame. Additional floor plane squares are generated from the initial square using the 45° VP as illustrated. This sketch also demonstrates how a cube maybe submerged beneath the floor plane. Fig. 4-17 shows a landscape scene which is drawn as a freehand sketch superimposed upon a grid. This allows accurate rendition of the area being represented.

Fig. 4-16

Perspective of 20/70 degree cube space from vanishing guide sketch frame:

Depth can be determined by square subdivision, or by using depth plane references as is done in one-point perspective. The cube "face diagonal" is used to generate elevated cubes as indicated with the dotted line. Note that final ground configuration need not be rectilinear, or on one level. The "plunged" cube could also have sloping sides as found in an embankment, and the irregular planting bed "undulates" against the wall.

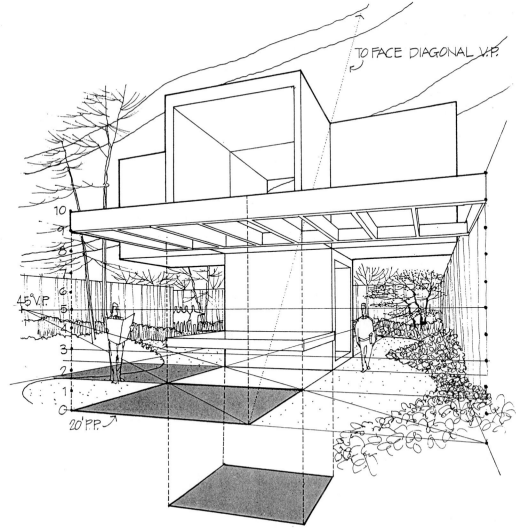

TO FACE DIAGONAL V.P.

45° V.P.

20' P.P.

10 9 8 7 6 5 4 3 2 1 0

Any perspective view can be changed in scale by using the scale multiplier method discussed in Chapter 3. Fig. 4-18 illustrates the reduction of a sketch frame to create an effective child's eye-view. It is also possible to enlarge the scale to create an aerial application, but a one-point aerial perspective might serve the same function and be easier to construct (See Fig. 3-16). In either a scale reduction or enlargement application, the same size initial 10' (3m) cube is drawn before the proportional distance values are decreased and increased respectively.

Fig. 4-17

A 20/70 degree vanishing guideline "freehand" sketching frame. An example of "plotting" a specific garden design over a reference grid.

Such a drawing may precede a plan view to encourage direct visualization of a design concept, or a preliminary visual fragment. Specific groupings of proposed plants may be drawn as shown to evaluate composition from various views. Once the system is mastered, the designer can always re-draw the image in plan because X, Y, and Z coordinates are transferable from the perspective. Spatial position and dimension are always known.

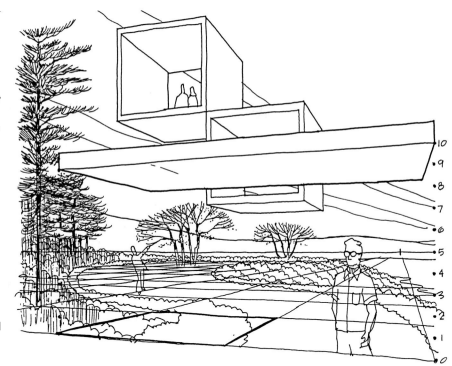

Fig. 4-18

A child's eye-view in 20/70 degree perspective from a 1/2 scale grid:

The reduced scale creates a 2.5' (0.75m) eye-level. Note that depth plane references are the same proportionally, as are those found in one-point perspective.

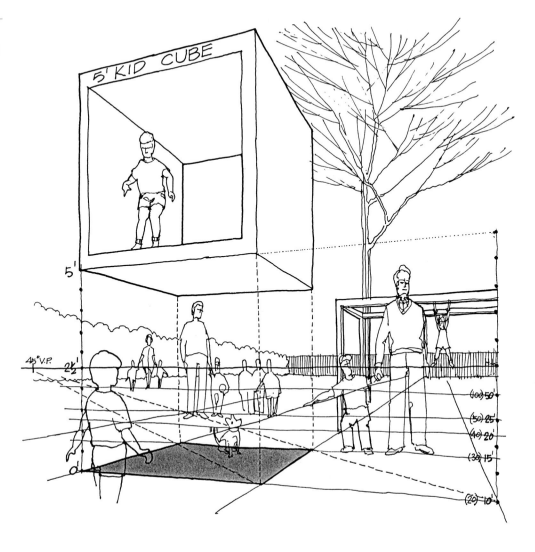

5

Three-Point Perspective

Three-point perspective theory

Three-point, or triaxial perspective, as the name implies, is a perspective view constructed with three vanishing points. It is usually applied to aerial perspective in landscape architecture, because the third vanishing point is generated by a "tilt" of the viewer's head, usually toward the ground from an aerial view. In three-point perspective, the viewer does not gaze off into the horizon, but instead focuses quite intently "up" or "down" at an object or into space, exemplified by the view in Fig. 5-1, which illustrates an aerial view of a three-point cube space, derived from an initial cube and scaled using the techniques described in Chapters 3 and 4.

The three-point perspective view has a very narrow cone of vision, and objects become unacceptably distorted very quickly at the peripheral edges. Its main virtue is its specific and focused point-of-view. Its main disadvantage, for the student, is the initial complexity of its construction. However, once its principles are learned, it is possible to develop a free-hand facility by constructing only minimal guidelines.

For the sake of continuity, the method of construction shown in the following figures are based upon an initial construction of a 30/60 degree floor grid, and its explanation has been shortened to emphasize the special features of three-point construction. It must be stated again however, that the triaxial measured perspective is more of a presentation tool than a quick, "in-process" design tool, but its fundamentals should be understood by the designer to ensure a full range of potential visualization methods. It is also the view that most computer-generated perspective views portray.

Fig. 5-1

A 30/60 degree three-point aerial perspective view of a large open space:
The initial cube has been divided so that each small square equals 10' (3m); the large cube is 100' (30m) square. There are no "vertical" lines since they converge at a third point, generated by a tilt of the viewer's head, as if observed from an airplane. Note that the "roof plane" of the sketch is actually the floor plane of a normal 30/60 degree perspective drawing, and that the cube is located "below" the ground surface plane.

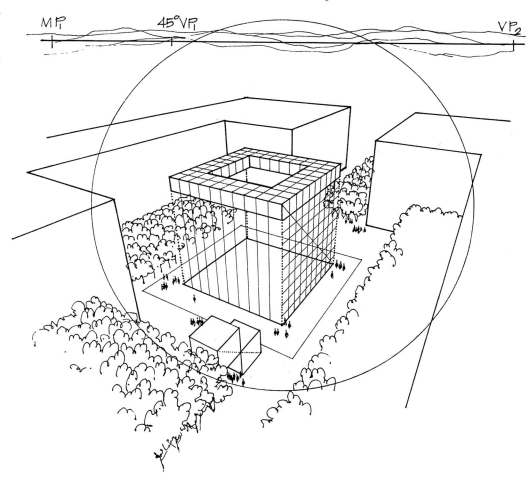

Figs. 5-1 and 5-2 illustrate the visual effect of changing the apparent scale of two identical cubes drawn in three-point perspective. The particular cubes shown were drawn by using the construction method outlined in this chapter. The top of the cube represents a 30/60 degree perspective square drawn so that the viewer is slightly higher than 5' in initial construction. The initial height of the viewer in relation to the top of the cube determines the downward angle of vision and the rate at which the "vertical" edges converge toward the third vanishing point. Fig. 5-2 shows the initial picture plane of the top cube surface indicated by a dashed line. The top front corner of the cube is touching the picture plane, and is the point at which all three perspective views converge.

If either Figs. 5-1 or 5-2 are turned in relation to the reader, so that each cube face is viewed as the "top" of another cube view, it will become apparent that a three-point perspective is actually the convergence of three separate two-point perspective views which share common vanishing points and which join at the three corners of the cube represented in the drawings.[26]

Fig. 5-2

A three-point perspective view showing initial cube at 5' (1.5m) scale:
Human figure height is taken from the cube and projected back to vanishing points. The same base drawing for this sketch was used to draw the view in Fig. 5-1.

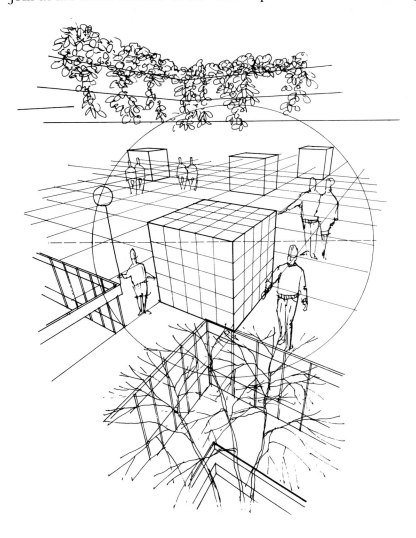

Construction methods

Step 1: Fig. 5-3 shows the first step in the construction of a three-point perspective view. The first step involves the construction of a 30/60 degree two-point perspective grid to establish an initial square as shown in the drawing inset. The construction shows the layout of a horizon line, its subdivision using 45 degree triangles and the establishment of a vertical scale slightly higher than normal. Raising the elevation of the viewer has the effect of sharpening the angle at which the viewer will be looking at the eventual cube as mentioned earlier. Using the scale established for the 5' (1.5m) eye-level, the picture plane is moved down to 8 units and centered at the intersection of the CV and the new PP, and a 10-unit circle is drawn to intersect the new PP. This arc establishes a 10-unit measuring dimension which will later be vanished back to the measuring point to locate the side of the initial square. An arc centered on HL is swung, from LVP to RVP, intersecting an extension of the CV line which is perpendicular to HL, to establish O.

Fig. 5-3

Initial set-up of 30/60 degree face of a three point perspective cube:
An initial construction diagram establishing the geometry of the top cube surface using 30/60 degree perspective construction technique (see Fig. 4-3). Note inset perspective showing effect of raising eye-level to see more of the cube surface. This diagram can also be used to create a normal two-point perspective with an eye-level slightly higher than the 5' (1.5m) used throughout this system.

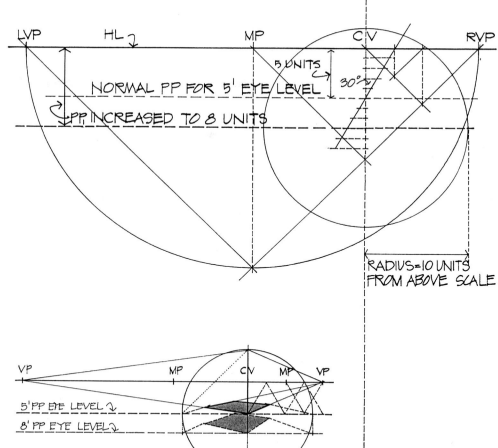

LVP HL MP CV RVP

5 UNITS
30°

NORMAL PP FOR 5' EYE LEVEL

PP INCREASED TO 8 UNITS

RADIUS=10 UNITS
FROM ABOVE SCALE

VP MP CV MP VP

5' PP EYE LEVEL
8' PP EYE LEVEL

DIAGRAM SHOWING EFFECT
OF INCREASING EYE LEVEL
TO 8' IN 30°-60° PERSPECTIVE

Step 2: Fig. 5-4 illustrates the next step in construction and can be best understood if studied in sequential fashion. From VP_1 and VP_2, draw CV_2 and CV_3 through A as shown. Through the intersections of CV_2 and CV_3 with a semi-circle, draw HL_2 and HL_3 to meet at VP_3. Draw an arc centered on VP_2 from O_1 to establish MP_1, and mark the intersection with CV_2 at O_2. Draw an arc centered on VP_3 from O_2 to locate MP_2, and mark the intersection with CV_3 at O_3. Draw an arc centered on VP_1 from O_3 to locate MP_3. Through A, draw PP_1 PP_2 and PP_3 parallel with the appropriate HL. The cube can now be constructed, one side at a time, using the intersection of the circle centered on A and each PP, as the dimension of the corresponding cube face edge.

Fig. 5-4

Second stage of construction of three-point perspective cube:
This stage establishes location of HL_2, HL_3, CV_2, CV_3, VP_3, MP_2, MP_3, PP_2, and PP_3. Circle at A intersects each PP to locate cube edge distance for each corresponding MP and HL. Point A represents the convergence of all three cube corners.

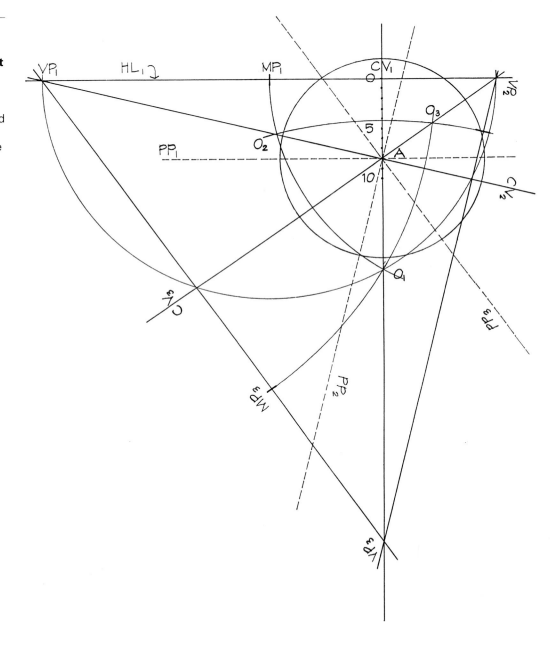

Fig. 5-5

Last stage of three-point construction:
Cube edges are vanished to MP₁, MP₂, and MP₃ and cube faces are outlined. Note dashed construction lines. Each HL can be viewed separately if drawing is turned accordingly. (See Figs. 5-7 and 5-8.)

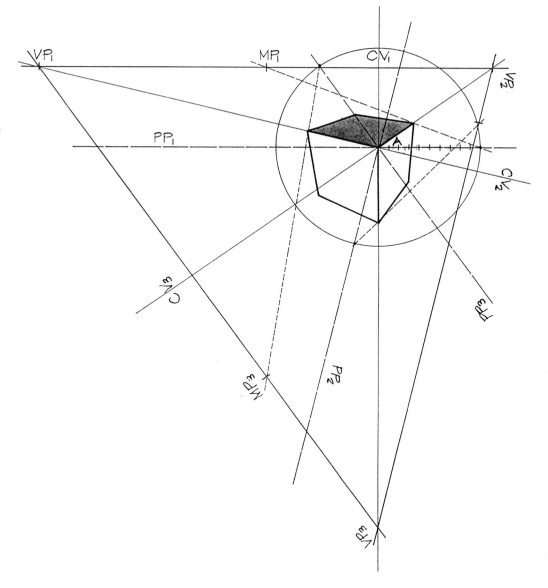

Step 3: Fig.5-5 shows the final step in constructing the initial cube. Each cube edge has been constructed by using the appropriate MP to vanish back the corresponding PP distance located by the circle centered at A. The circle is 10 units in diameter and is transferred to the sides with the dashed lines shown. A detail of this process is shown in Fig. 5-6. It further illustrates how

Fig. 5-6

Enlarged detail of scaling technique using MPs: Concentric rings intersect PPs to establish scale increments (10 units), which in turn are vanished back to the corresponding MP to locate the increments on the appropriate cube edge (after Walters & Bromham).

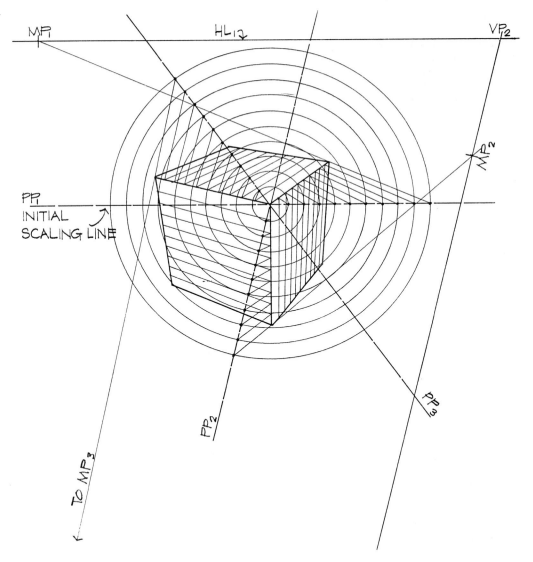

the cube can be divided into unit increments by transferring them from the PP via MP. Each cube face can be scribed with a grid by vanishing the transferred increments, back to the three VPs. Figs. 5-7 and 5-8 show how each cube face appears as the corresponding HL is positioned horizontally.

The only true vertical in the perspective falls on the CV, which by definition is perpendicular to HL. Once the three VPs are established, all drawing is done with one straight edge. There is no need for a parallel bar or T-square. After a cube has been drawn and has been divided into square grid units, a small sketch may be drawn "into" the cube and then photographically enlarged to make a large drawing with a unique view. The drawing can then be rendered with a free hand technique.

Fig. 5-7

Three-point perspective showing side two as the reference ground plane.
Note the shaded initial 30/60 degree square.

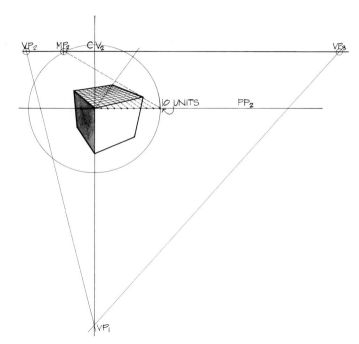

Fig. 5-8

Three-point perspective showing side three as the reference ground plane:
Initial square is shaded. This view is very effective for looking down into a court-yard which has many level changes. The sketch should not be allowed outside of the circle. This view is good for vertical depth because the cube is located so high in the visual cone.

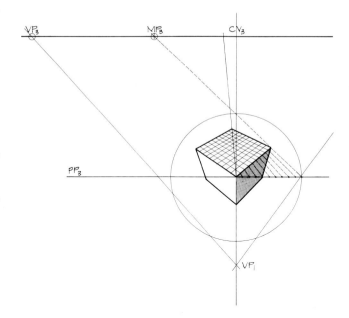

Once drawn, the cube views can be saved to serve as "perspective charts" and sketch frame guides for future reference. Chapter 9 illustrates computer-generated versions of each of these views, which may be used as perspective grid sketch frames.

6

Spatial Cross-Sections

Design Cross-Section

The design cross-section is the second most common design drawing technique used by landscape architects for all phases of work. It is second only to the plan view in application to most design problems. As the name implies, the cross-section represents a "cut" or "slice" through the subject being studied or illustrated. A cross-section view is a cut which is perpendicular to a longitudinal axis. In landscape architecture, a cross-section view is used to illustrate a variety of subjects at many different scales.

Fig. 6-1 illustrates a number of cross-section views.

1. The cut line of a cross-section is usually a heavy dark line to emphasize the configuration of the section surface, and to differentiate the cut line from other lines not within the section view.

2. A construction cross-section is used to indicate the thickness of materials, the manner in which different materials are joined or attached, and other such information necessary for fabrication and installation. Such detail cross-sections are usually drawn at scales ranging from 1/2 "=l'-0" (1:20) to 3"=1'-0" (1 : 5) and in some cases are drawn to true 1 : 1 scale.

3. A site planning design cross-section is used to illustrate structure/ground relationships to assess the effects of grading on existing slopes and vegetation, to illustrate design standards and criteria, or to present design concepts. Scales appropriate for this type of section range from 1/8 "=1'-0" (1:100) to 1/32 "=1'-0" (1:200-1:500).

Fig. 6-1

Construction, design, and illustrative sections:
Views of various cross-section applications to illustrate typical landscape architecture issues and design concepts: (1) heavy line at section cut; (2) detail view; (3) site design section; (4) concept section. Section views are absolutely essential for understanding plan drawings, and help to augment perspective sketches as well.

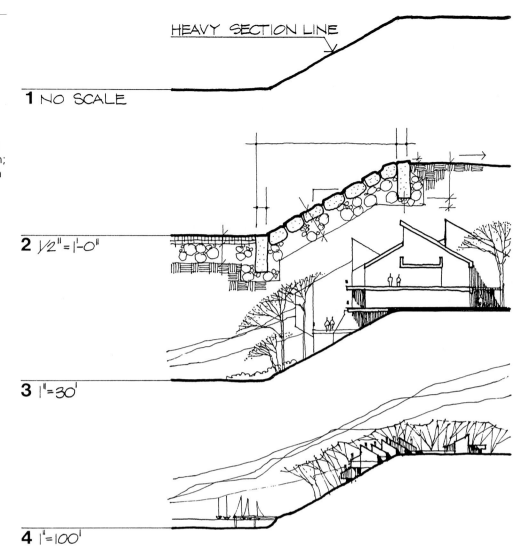

HEAVY SECTION LINE

1 NO SCALE

2 1/2" = 1'-0"

3 1" = 30'

4 1" = 100'

4. Large scale illustrative sections are used to assess and explain site analysis and design concepts, or site organization concepts; to illustrate vertical use relationships; and generally to indicate proposed site use and activity distribution. In the sections shown (1-4), all are articulated with a strong ground or cut line and have a gradation of line weight to draw attention to the foreground and to allow the background to recede.[27]

The cross-section view in landscape architecture is absolutely essential for understanding the implications of a plan drawing, which as mentioned in Chapter 1, is merely a scaled diagram with encoded spatial and volumetric information.

■ *The section view, like the perspective view, can add important visual design analysis data to the design process by testing and documenting viewer lines of sight and perception thresholds of distance and enclosure.*[28]

It is an important adjunct to the perspective view, which when viewed together, creates a more complete understanding of the spatial "potential" of a particular design.

Fig. 6-2

Typical "sketch-section" graphics executed in soft pencil:
Note line weight hierarchy and shade gradation. The 5' (1.5m) eye-level line creates a section "sketch frame."

Fig. 6-2 presents graphic techniques suggested for small scale design study sections. Human figures add scale and animation to a cross-section view. When figures are used for such purposes, they should be animated and engaged in activities associated with the theme of the cross-section. Studies such as those shown in Fig. 6-2 are typically used in preliminary design stages, and can be drawn freehand to a relative scale.

The top sketch shows horizontal guidelines which are drawn at 5' (1.5m) eye-level, 30" (0.75m) table level, and 15" (0.37m) seating level, so that figures may be sketched freely and still remain in scale. This "cross-section sketch

6 Spatial Cross-Sections

74

frame" is very similar to the one-point perspective sketch frames illustrated in Chapter 3.

Familiarity with the human scale environment as revealed in such section studies makes it easier to imagine and to execute such environments in perspective drawings, especially if using the depth plane reference system, in which each depth plane can be viewed to represent an "elevation/section" drawing. In its simplest form, a one-point perspective may be viewed as a series of individual overlapping cross-section/elevation drawings seen simultaneously as if all were drawn on clear acetate film.

Fig. 6-3

Design section detail at 1/4 = 1'-0" (1:50):
A typical study of building, vegetation, and ground relationships. Since most of the attention is to be focused on the ground line, it is given the heaviest weight. The building cross-section is drawn with a dark outline, but without tone, to allow visual attention to be focused on the ground line. This cross-section is drawn to scale with a straight edge and soft pencil. The drawing techniques used in this section are also used in one-point perspective drawings.

Fig. 6-4

Typical "line section" to show grading and planting relationship:
Note use of cars and people for scale reference.
(after Johnson)

GROUND OR "CUT" LINE

Figs. 6-4 and 6-5 show a general cross-section view, appropriate for the purpose of illustrating land form and subtle grading concepts. General cross-section views such as these are particularly important for those situations involving considerable elevation changes. In such instances, it is effective to show a continuous "mural-type" of cross-section through a very significant part of the site being studied. The long linear drawing could be drawn on one continuous sheet of vellum, or drawn on smaller sheets and spliced together, either before or after printing. This type of cross-section can be used for illustrating design proposals, or for analyzing the site.

Fig. 6-5 shows how a cross-section may be combined with a one-point perspective to show two types of information simultaneously.[29]

Illustrative and technical sections

The design section in the design development stage is often a pre-construction drawing that must contain both the spirit of place as well as the needed technical data to insure physical feasibility and to illustrate measurable performance criteria (design simulation). Fig. 6-6 represents a cross-section technique drawn to a scale of 1"=20' (1:200), and is used to illustrate the design standards of the parking lot above. Such cross-sections when labeled and dimensioned become valuable supplements to plan presentations because they not only show ground plane undulations, but also illustrate mass and void relationships. Often cross-sections like that illustrated in Fig. 6-6 can be "keyed" to the larger general section, in the same manner that a construction detail is keyed to a layout plan. It is, in effect, a larger scale design construction section and informs the viewer of basic dimensions.

Fig. 6-6

Use of cross-section to present planning and design standards for a proposed design:
Section shows ground plane undulations and canopy and enclosure elements, which are merely implied in plan.

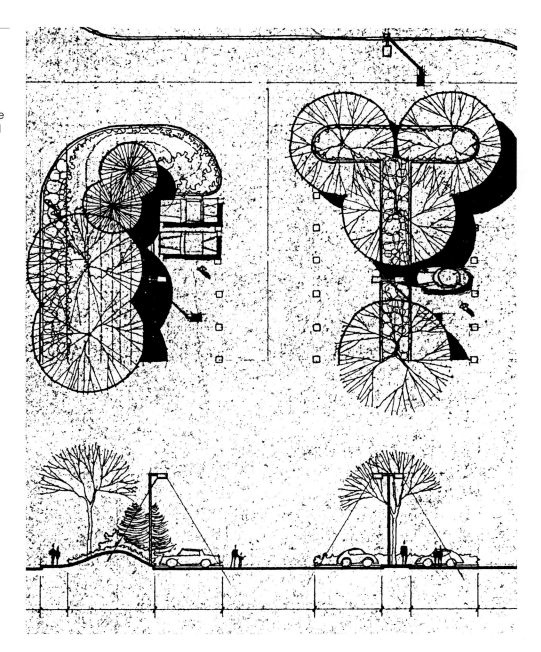

Fig. 6-7

Illustrative section keyed to more detailed sections: The overall section visually and numerically summarizes the design concept, while at the same time serving to direct attention to more detailed construction drawings for individual design elements. The large section serves as a context for the design materials and methods of construction in a manner difficult to duplicate in plan view alone.

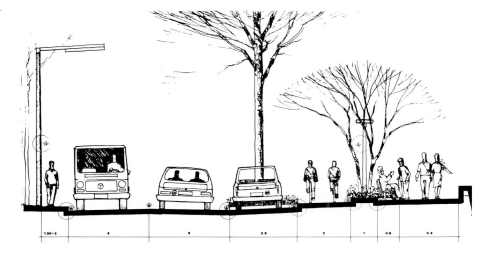

Fig. 6-7 illustrates such an application within a general illustrative section. In this instance, the general section shown in Fig. 6-7 indicates the site location and the reference number or symbol of construction detail drawings, but with a much clearer sense of both design intent and construction context than is typically found in a plan reference system. Fig. 6-8, illustrates still another example of how design sections may serve multiple roles in the design process. The figure indicates existing conditions (existing and proposed grades, major vegetation, and structures), the proposed construction elements, and give a sense of the potential outcome to both the designer and client, and to the contractor. Such information is also vital to producing more detailed perspective presentation drawings. The sections all show human figures engaged in the activities associated with the place being studied, and therefore help the viewer to further grasp the meaning of the design, much more effectively than do traditionally drawn plans.

Fig. 6-8

A technical section used for construction, illustrative, and design analysis purposes:
The sections show existing and proposed elements as well as the human intention as indicated by the scale figures.

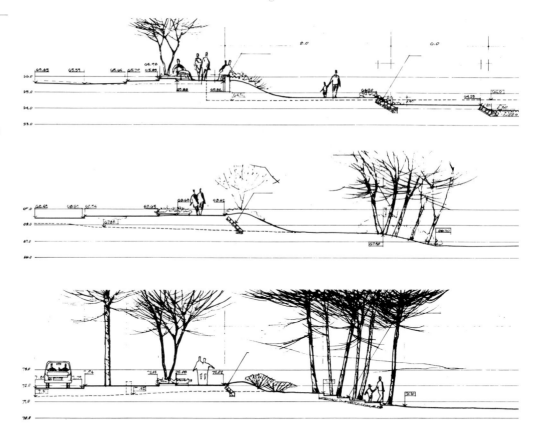

Planting design requires the use of cross-section and elevation views to illustrate the massing effects of proposed plantings. Fig. 6-9 shows such a section/elevation view applied to architecture, where depth is accomplished through line weight differences, overlap, and building shadows. Such a drawing style illustrates the proposed plantings at mature growth stages to permit a view of the final composition, which informs the perspective study sketch. Fig. 6-10 illustrates how a section/elevation is applied to a proposal for a memorial garden composed of landform, vegetation, and stones. The human figures locate the pathways and provide a sense of landform scale. Such a drawing augments the viewer's understanding of the plan image.

Fig. 6-9

Example of section/ elevation view used for planting design study: All heights are true scale and depth is only indicated by building shadow and line weight hierarchy. A well-drawn elevation is like a depth layer in a one-point perspective drawing.

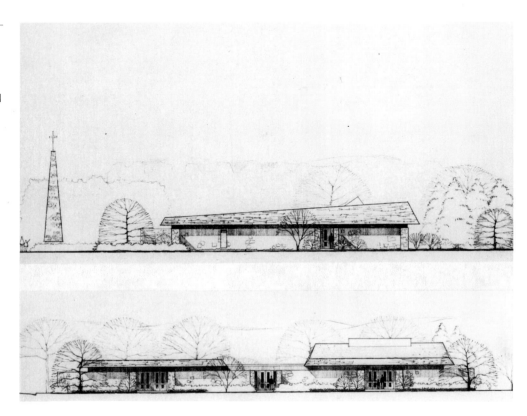

Fig. 6-10

Planting plan and section/ elevation of a memorial park:

The scale figures locate the walkways and provide a scaling reference for both the mature plantings and the landforms. Depth is achieved by merely overlapping plant mass outlines; such a simple technique does not require heavy rendering because "overlap" is such a primary visual cue for depth.

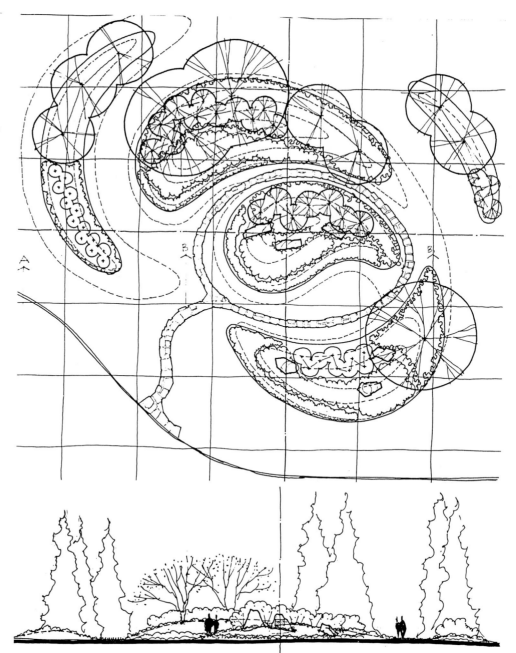

Fig. 6-11

Drawing techniques for a design development cross-section study:

The techniques used in such a section are similar to those found in the 40' (12m) to 60' (18m) depth range of a one-point perspective view. Technical elements such as spot elevations, footing depths, special planting conditions, etc., are easily combined with an illustrative style for maximum visual stimulation and design content.

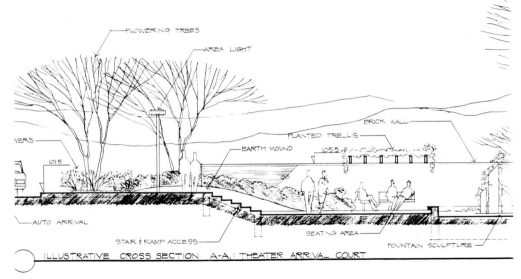

ILLUSTRATIVE CROSS SECTION A-A: THEATER ARRIVAL COURT

Fig. 6-11 summarizes a number of common techniques used to represent design development sections which help the designer simulate spatial and dimensional aspects.

Section/perspective

A cross-section drawn at the 20' (6m) picture plane (PP) may be vanished back in normal one-point perspective construction for a more informative section detail as shown in Fig. 6-12. The section/perspective gives all of the information shown in Fig. 6-8, plus the spirit found in Fig. 6-11, as well as the spatial content of a single perspective view.

The drawing in Fig. 6-12 shows a construction detail of an an ornamental water feature and surrounding fence, but the content has been augmented by the perspective sketch, which informs both client and contractor. It serves as an evaluative drawing for the designer (the full plans for this garden can be seen in Fig. 7-8, Chapter 7).

Fig. 6-12

Section/perspective view of a water garden:
The construction section is drawn at the 20' (6m) picture plane, and the garden is drawn as a one-point perspective to give contextual meaning to the client and contractor, while providing a design assessment tool for the designer.

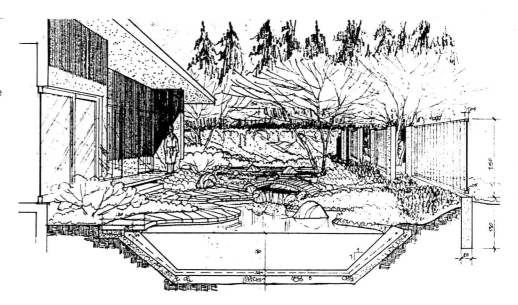

Fig. 6-13

A form of a section/ perspective view without the explicit initial section at the picture plane:
The elevated eye-level creates a broad overview of the proposed concept; the rendering style indicates the sectional landscape properties; and the human figures convey the design intent and its scale relationships.

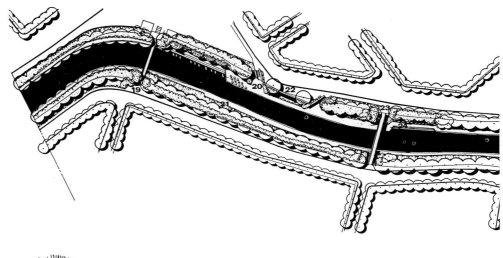

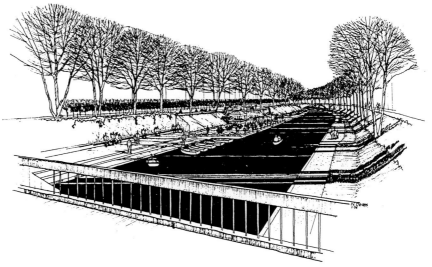

Another form of a section/perspective drawing is illustrated by Fig. 6-13, which shows a design concept for a linear river walk park. Although the perspective is not drawn as a section, it is rendered in a style that accentuates the sectional properties of the design concept through the use of shadows, and an elevated view from a bridge. The plan above represents the elements shown in the perspective view: the viewing bridge at (19), the river cafe and plaza at (20), the pedestrian walks at (21) and (24). In contrast to the perspective drawing shown in Fig. 6-13, is a normal section view of a proposed pedestrian bridge for another location in the river park corridor shown in Fig. 6-14. Both the perspective and the section views depict the same basic information: level change, existing trees (*populous caroliniana*), channel width, pedestrian activity, etc., but the perspective conveys far more design content than the rather stark section in Fig. 6-14.

Fig. 6-14

Normal site section at a point downstream from the view in Fig. 6-13:
Although this section addresses the same information as does the perspective in Fig. 6-13, it does not contain the depth of design content conveyed by the perspective view.

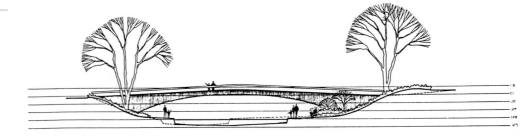

Parallel and
Plan Projections

Parallel projection is a method of drawing which is not used often enough by landscape architects for exploring three-dimensional aspects of design ideas. It is a good alternative to perspective for beginning students because of its ease of construction, and its dimensional accuracy and accountability. There are many types of parallel projection, but the two most useful for the landscape architect are the Planometric and Axonometric projections.

Planometric projections

Planometric projection is a general term that includes all projections of scaled plans which have been tipped to a specific angle and projected vertically to form a third dimension. Planometric projections vary by the angle of plan tilt. Fig. 7-1 shows three typical planometric views: (1) the 60/30 degree, 1:1:1 side ratio projection; (2) the 30/60 degree, 1:2:2 side ratio projection; and (3) the 45/45 degree, 1:1:1 side ratio projection.[30] In each case, the top square is in true plan. Planometric projections are good for technical illustrations such as construction drawings and are very easy to draw, but are rather severe in appearance for spatial design studies. Other projection methods are more conducive to spatial analysis and are presented below.

Axonometric projections

Axonometric is a general term for projected views of objects which have no true plan view and the sides of which are all inclined with respect to the horizontal reference plane. The axonometric view has a more "natural appearance" than the planometric view and is therefore much more valuable as an illustrative tool for landscape architects. The most common and easy to use of the axonometric views is the isometric projection illustrated in drawing 4 of Fig. 7-1. The isometric projection is drawn with a 30/60 degree triangle, using equal (iso) angles, and all sides are drawn to true scale to achieve a 1:1:1 side scale ratio. The isometric projection view has a high potential for illustrating landscape space, especially when rendered with shadows and texture.

Fig. 7-1

Planometric and axonometric parallel projection:
The types most suitable for landscape architecture are 30/60 degree planometric and 30/30 degree isometric. Isometric is very effective as a substitute for perspective, and can often be used for pre-perspective studies. Such drawings contain plan, elevation, and volumetric information.

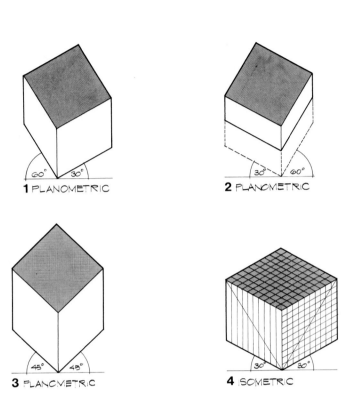

1 PLANOMETRIC

2 PLANOMETRIC

3 PLANOMETRIC

4 ISOMETRIC

Fig. 7-2 illustrates a hypothetical planting and grading study viewed in isometric projection. The drawing illustrates how plan and cross-section information can be plotted with a scale. Such a drawing is also helpful for studying shadow behavior, which in turn may be applied to perspective drawings. To draw effectively, careful attention must be paid to line weight hierarchy so that the outline of an object is of a distinctly different value than the edge of an object. This can be observed in Fig. 7-2.

Fig. 7-2

Application of isometric projection to evaluate a design:
Note how effectively contours can be plotted and studied with this view. Isometric is also good for shadow analysis.

The isometric view is effective for small vignettes, but is very time consuming for whole site plans. These views work best when illustrating a detailed design segment which needs quick three-dimensional analysis. Once accustomed to this view, a designer may develop an accurate free-hand sketch technique to compensate for the more intricate drafting requirements of isometric drawings. Their main virtue is that they are true scale three-dimensional representations of design ideas, and simulate many of the same relationships found in simple scale massing models.

Plan projections

The art of shadow projection, referred to technically as sciagraphy, is a precise form of descriptive geometry.[31] It is based upon theories concerning the behavior of light, both solar and artificial, cast upon various geometric solids and tipped planes. The purpose of the following presentation is to focus upon those aspects of shadow projection which are more directly linked to design drawing for illustrative purposes, rather than upon a detailed investigation of technically precise shadow projection.

■ *In design drawing, shadows create illusions of visual depth, and articulate the planar relationship of surfaces adjacent to one another.*

Shadows also serve to highlight objects and areas by providing contrasting tonal values. The illustrations in this chapter and in other parts of the book show shadow projection techniques for plans, parallel projections, one- and two-point perspectives, elevations and cross-sections, and freehand design drawings.

Fig. 7-3

Illustrations of shadow projections for various methods of three-dimensional simulation drawing:
(l) one-point perspective
(2) three-point perspective
(3) plan view
(4) isometric projection;
(5) cross-section/elevation.

Shadows in (1), (2), and (4) have been constructed from plan view in (3).

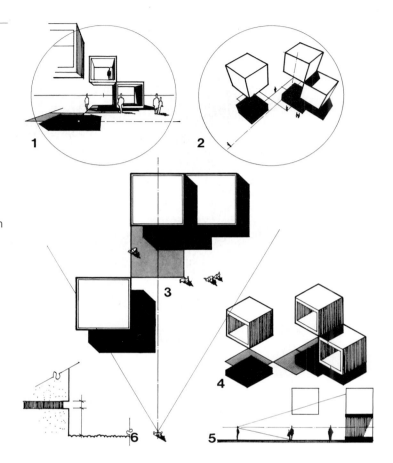

Fig. 7-3 illustrates the effects of shadow projections on the key design simulation drawing types described earlier in Chapter 1. Plan shadow projection technique, which in essence is a form of planometric projection, is a fundamental skill in landscape site plan drawing.

The most commonly applied and easy to use three-dimensional simulation technique is the 45 degree shadow projection of plan elements. Such a plan projection is an oblique projection, with shadows being cast by all vertical plan elements at a 45 degree angle from the upper left or upper right hand plan corner. Drawing 3, in Fig. 7-3, illustrates the projection effect. The illusion of depth occurs because of tonal value gradation (a primary visual cue), and because of the oblique projection geometry.

Shadow projection for illustrative purposes should not be confused with shadow projections drawn for solar ground shadow analysis, which is a function of building orientation in relation to the sun. Such an analysis is used in urban design and site planning to study building massing and ground shadow patterns. These technical analyses, although correct in regard to actual sun shadows, serve a very specialized purpose and are, in most cases, not useful as plan illustrations.

Illustrative plan shadows are usually projected from the upper left hand, or right hand corner to the opposite lower corner of the drawing, for the same reason that aerial photographs, before being viewed stereoscopically, are always arranged so that shadows fall from top to bottom, regardless of north orientation. In this arrangement, the stereoscopic illusion of depth is maximized. If turned, so that shadows point to the top of the photo, depressions appear to be mounds, and mounds appear to be depressions.

■ *Black and generally dark tones tend to appear as depressions or water bodies, and light to white tones tend to be interpreted as representing high points.*

This phenomenon can be seen while flying in an airplane and viewing the landscape below. Drier, high soil areas appear to be lighter than the river and stream valleys, which are, in most cases, darker green and deeper in shadow.

Fig. 7-4 is a composite of typical shadow projection conditions encountered in landscape architecture plan renderings. The gradation of black and white values is an important part of this drawing. Areas left completely white are more prominent than those which have been toned with a textural shading effect. An area in white, when sharply contrasted with black or a very deep tone, becomes especially highlighted. Grey tones are used to neutralize floor plane elements such as pavements, grass, and ground cover, so that lighter canopies of trees and edges of structures will have a contrasting value.

The shadow length indicates the heights of plan elements, relative to one another. Vertical edges such as wall corners and poles, cast lines at a 45 degree angle, the length of which is usually established by visual judgment, but may be established by cross-section and elevation analysis; typically the object height to shadow length ratio is 1:1 or 1: 0.8. Horizontal planes, or edges such as building overhangs, tops of walls, umbrellas, tables, etc., cast area shadows, the outline of which is a 45 degree projection of the true plan configuration.

■ *Actual shadow length on the drawing is less important than relative length.*

If shadow length is too extreme, the shadows will obscure valuable plan information. If they are too shallow, the depth illusion will be minimized. In cases where a plan is heavily detailed and rich in ground plane information, shadows can be shaded with a transparent shading film, allowing pavement patterns and textures to be clearly read. This technique is usually required when large building shadows shade an area.

The specific techniques for expressing various plan projection conditions are indicated by the numbered areas in Fig. 7- 4, and are described as follows:

1. The automobile, treated as a slab floating above the pavement, is not connected to the shadow at its outside corners, which are offset at 45 degrees.

Fig. 7-4

An anthology of typical shadow projection techniques used to express various site conditions:

1. auto

2. steps with end wall sloping with step descent

3. steps with end wall horizontal at constant level, making shadow longer at lower end

4. small structure with overhang

5. people engaged in various activities

6. material, textures, and tones

7. water splash effect

8. people "engulfed" in shadow

9. earth mound shading for contour expression

10. light pole and globe light fixture

11. tables and umbrellas

12. overlapping trees casting shadows on each other

2. Shadows cast on steps by the top of a wall which is parallel to the angle of the step descent follow the projection of the sloping surface intercepted by the horizontal steps (see detail in Fig. 7-6).

3. Shadows cast by a wall plane edge which is parallel to the step surface are expressed as a horizontal line. As the steps go down, the shadow grows longer (the wall gets higher), and therefore covers more of the stairway. The riser of each tread is emphasized by a small shadow line in both (2) and (3).

4. Small structures with an overhang cast shadows which reflect the "floating" overhang shape, and the "pole" effect of of the vertical edge which supports it.

5. People cast shadows which reflect their activities. People walking allow light to pass between their legs, and those engaged in animated conversation will cast shadows with their arms (see Fig. 7-6).

6. Textured surfaces, besides indicating materials, also result in a tone. The symbol shown can mean cobblestone, exposed aggregate, or some other such "non-directional" pavement expression.

7. Water fountains can be expressed boldly by contrasting the white spray of water with a black water pool.

8. It is effective to show people at the edge of, and engulfed by, shadows of large trees or buildings, because it contributes a sense of movement and human activity. It also intensely highlights the human figure.

9. Topographic mounding and slope in general can be expressed by shading the side in shadow with a variety of techniques, and by casting a shadow produced by a horizontal element like a tree "canopy" or building roof edge, which will express the slope, much as the steps do in (3).

10. Lamp posts and spheres will appear as lines and circles when projected in plan.

11. Small tables and umbrellas cast their plan shape projected at 45 degrees.

12. Trees grouped together can be expressed as overlapping one another by casting partial shadows to reflect the rounded quality of the adjacent tree crown. (This is further illustrated in Fig. 7-7).

Fig. 7-5

Illustrative Plan:
Example of illustrative plan
used for local planning board
presentation (note use of
graphics and words).

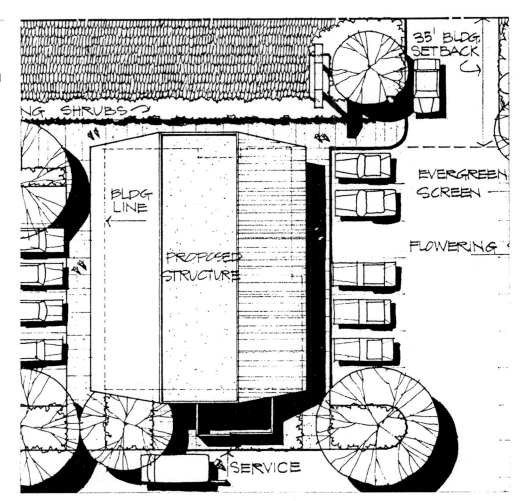

Fig. 7-5 illustrates the general application of these techniques to an illustrative site plan of a proposed restaurant for submission to a local planning board. It illustrates through both shadows and words the proposed sign location, an auto drop-off area, parking, walls, fences, and service access (see truck in rear). The drawing also illustrates the technique of allowing certain elements such as fences, walls, people, and cars to "pop" through shadows, when covering them would obscure an important idea or concept. This has the effect of highlighting the object emerging from the shadows.

Fig. 7-6 illustrates some of the details found in Fig. 7-4. Drawing (1) is a very detailed treatment of people sitting, reading, talking, and walking. Actually, representing people from plan view is almost an obscure art form by itself, but one which adds content to any detailed plan. (Note how bench is allowed to be outlined in white at its lower right edge). Drawing (2) illustrates the principle of shadows being cast by a floating slab in both plan and perspective views. Because the plan shadow is cast at 45 degrees, the 45° VP is used to project the shadow displacement in perspective, shown by the dashed lines. (Note that the vertical angle of the sun will intercept a vertical projection of the 45° VP.) Drawings (3) and (4) illustrate how shadows fall in 45 degree plan projection over steps and inclined planes in general.

For plan graphics, it is not necessary to be absolutely accurate with projections in such cases, because the purpose is to show the fact of level change, and not its precise nature. If more precise presentations are required, then enlarged plans, cross-sections, and isometric projections should be used.

Fig. 7-6

Details of plan shadow techniques:

1. people sitting, standing, talking

2. canopy shadow projection in plan and projection

3. shadows on steps with wall horizontal

4. shadows on steps with wall sloping.

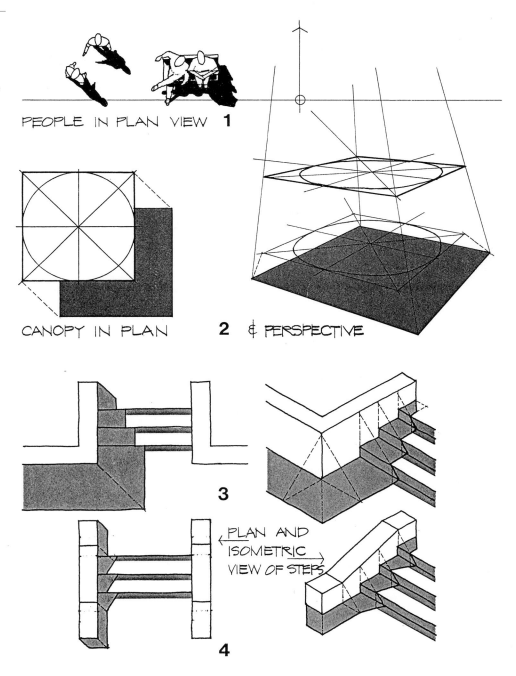

PEOPLE IN PLAN VIEW 1

CANOPY IN PLAN

2 ¢ PERSPECTIVE

3

4

←PLAN AND ISOMETRIC VIEW OF STEPS→

Fig. 7-7

Plan of villa and garden showing indoor-outdoor rooms:
This plan shows only diagrammatically the spatial arrangements of plan elements, and requires detailed explanation of three-dimensional implications.

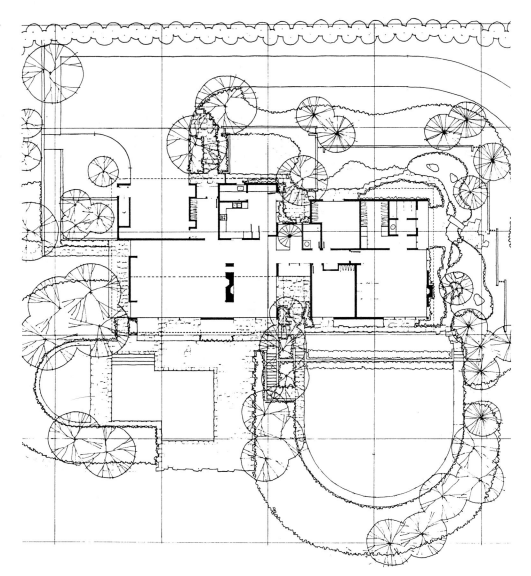

Fig. 7-8

Plan of villa in Fig. 7-7 showing shadows to imply depths and illustrate elements of spatial enclosure:
The water garden is illustrated in the section/perspective shown in Fig. 6-12.

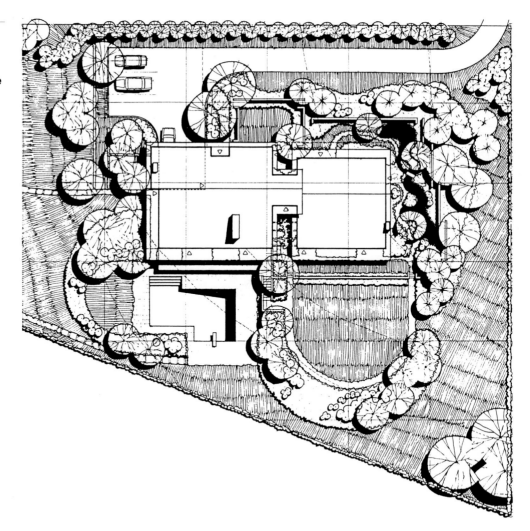

Figs. 7-7 and 7-8 demonstrate how shadow projections alter the apparent content of a simple line drawing. The unrendered plan shown in Fig. 7-7 is really little more than a diagrammatic expression of the design's spatial potential, but it does show very clearly the indoor-outdoor relationship of architecture and garden. The shadows cast in Fig. 7-8 transform a two-dimensional base plan into a simulated three-dimensional model. The water garden seen in this plan appears as a section/perspective in Fig. 6-12.

Fig. 7-9

Rendered illustrative plan of an office building and parking garage at 1" = 100' (1:1000):
A typical technique used to express building and vegetation massing, implied topographic changes, and major circulation systems. The line weights "contain" the graphic content of each plan element. The shadow lengths are slightly less than 1:1.

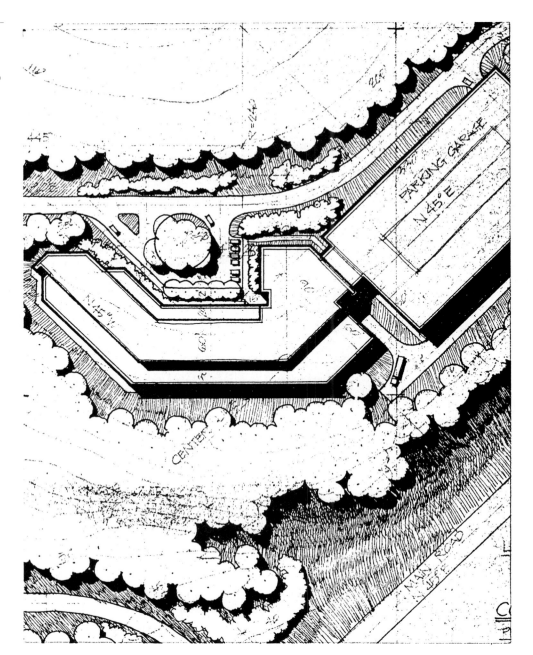

Plan shadow projections of the type shown in Fig. 7-9 are especially useful in schematic design sketch plan drawings for quickly assessing the spatial sense of a proposed scheme. The loading dock area, and the space between the parking garage and the "main road" demonstrate how tonal shading of the ground plane can simulate existing or proposed grade changes and slopes. Fig. 7-10 offers another example of site plan sketch graphics drawn at the same scale as Fig. 7-9, and shows about the same amount of detail.

Fig. 7-10

Rendered illustrative plan of an office park:
This general plan is drawn at the same scale as Figure 7-9. A detail of its entrance features appears in Figure 7-11.

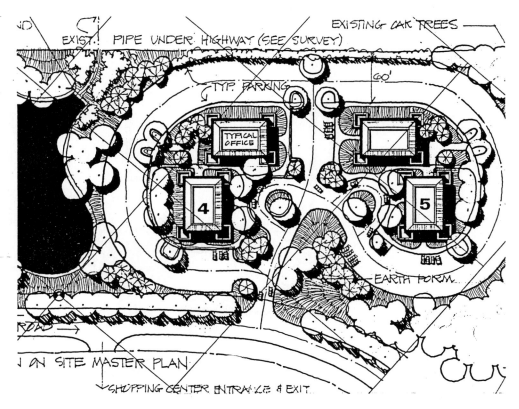

Design development drawings require a different technique because more detail must be shown. Fig. 7-11 shows a schematic design development drawing at 1/16" = 1'-0" (1:200) of a building arrival area taken from Fig. 7-10, in which paving patterns, walls, and a finer level of planting design are illustrated. The shadows are used to engulf and to highlight critical details, and to convey a degree of relative depths for various plan elements (note how tops of walls and people emerge from the shadows around the building).

Fig. 7-11

Detail of office park concept plan showing site design elements:
This plan uses line weight gradations and deep shadows to gain maximum depth illusion. By allowing trees to "pop" out of the building shadows, they serve to illuminate the ground plane pattern and to outline walls and fences. The plan also indicates minimum dimension standards. Note people entering upper building as they walk into the shadows. The plan is drawn at 1/16" = 1'-0" (1:200).

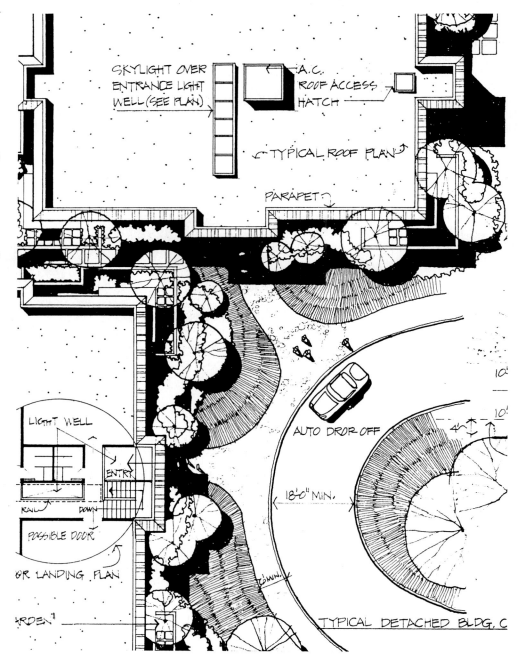

SKYLIGHT OVER ENTRANCE LIGHT WELL (SEE PLAN)

A.C. ROOF ACCESS HATCH

TYPICAL ROOF PLAN

PARAPET

LIGHT WELL

ENTRY

RAIL   DOWN

POSSIBLE DOOR

OR LANDING PLAN

RDEN

AUTO DROP-OFF

18'-0" MIN.

10'

10'

4'

DOWN

TYPICAL DETACHED BLDG. C

Fig. 7-12

Rendered design development plan of a large villa showing all site elements:
This pre-construction drawing contains the layout, grading, drainage, planting, site structure, and spatial information required to create production drawings. It also implies a spatial quality that is verified in perspective views, such as shown in Fig. 7-13.

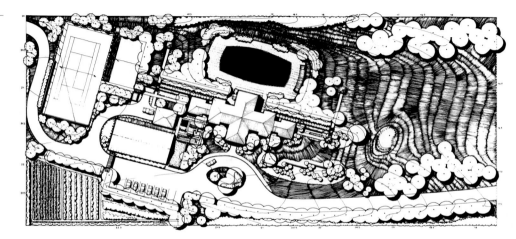

Fig. 7-13

Perspective view of villa arrival circle:
The sketch is one of a series done to explore the spatial implications of the proposed design elements shown in Fig. 7-12.

Figs. 7-12 and 7-13 represent a traditional relationship between rendered plan and illustrative perspective. They provide an opportunity to assess the comparison of the impression produced by the plan view of the auto arrival circle and that produced by the perspective sketch of the same area from the user's point-of-view. Fig. 7-13 is one of a series of sketch vignettes that were produced to simulate the spatial aspects of the design, and to correct the plan drawing when appropriate.

Fig. 7-14

Plan, elevation, and perspective shadow studies:
A shadow study of a cube structure showing shadow projections in plan (Plans 1-4), elevation (Views 1-3), and in two-point perspective showing light source in front of viewer. Note how line weights and shadows help to differentiate between mass and void.

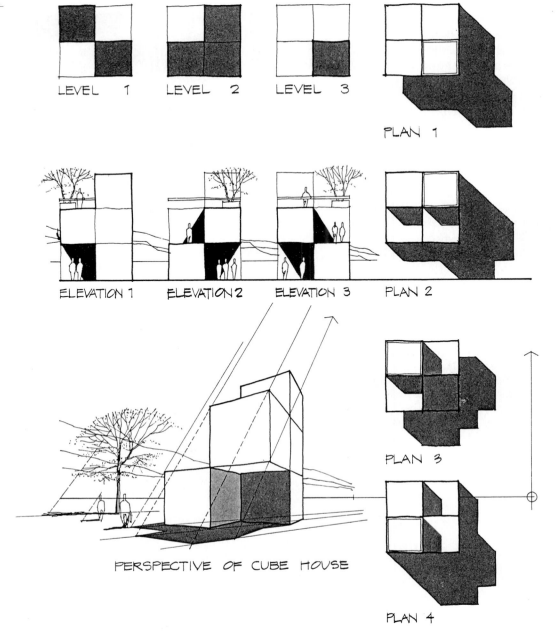

LEVEL 1   LEVEL 2   LEVEL 3

PLAN 1

ELEVATION 1   ELEVATION 2   ELEVATION 3   PLAN 2

PLAN 3

PERSPECTIVE OF CUBE HOUSE

PLAN 4

Perspective shadow projection

Fig. 7-14 illustrates the combination of plan, elevation, and perspective shadow projection used to visually analyze an arrangement of cubes in a 4-square, 3-level composition expressed in plan by views of each level (1, 2, and 3), and elevations of three sides (elevations 1, 2, and 3). Plan shadows are cast by rotating the composition 90° for each plan rendition (1, 2, 3, and 4), thus implying by shadow alone which cubes are high, and which cubes are low. The elevations are shaded using a 30/60° triangle to cast shadows of cube overhangs to indicate which cubes are in the foreground and which ones are in the background. Heavy lines are also used to denote foreground cubes.

The series of plans, elevations, and perspective view together reveal the complexities of the cube composition. This simple exercise illustrates the importance of shadow projections in three-dimensional design simulation drawings.

The perspective drawing in Fig. 7-14 illustrates a typical method for projecting shadows in two point perspective, using a light source in front and to the right of the viewer.[32] Solar rays are assumed to be parallel as they strike the earth's surface, and therefore cast horizontal shadows which are also parallel.

■ *In perspective, all parallel lines converge to points on the horizon or to slope points above or below it.*

To cast shadows in perspective, two points are required. The first point locates the light source vanishing point (LSVP), and the second point locates the shadow vanishing point (SVP), which represents the point on the horizon line toward which all solar produced floor plane shadows vanish. Usually, the shadow vanishing point is located away from either the LVP or the RVP to avoid confusion when projecting ground line shadows.

In the case presented in Fig. 7-14, the subject is "backlit" by the sun and the light source projector point is located above the horizon (see arrow direction in perspective drawing). This point should be very "high" above the HL to achieve a more natural sunlight effect. This height is determined by visual judgement. If the sun angle is too low, the resultant shadows will be elongated and exaggerated. In Fig. 7-14, the shadow vanishing point (SVP) has been located to the right of the perspective RVP and the light source projector point is directly above it (see arrow).

Shadow projector lines are first drawn on the ground plane by projecting from the structure base corners, lines radiating away from the shadow vanishing point (SVP). Next, lines projecting from the light source projector are drawn to connect the top corners of buildings, overhangs, people, trees, poles, etc., and to intercept the previously-drawn shadow projectors. At the intersection of the two lines so constructed, lines are vanished back to the LVP and RVP to construct the top edges of building and structures as reflected on the floor plane. For poles, posts, trees, etc., the intersection on the ground plane merely marks the length of the shadow. A "front-lit" shadow effect is achieved by placing the light source vanishing point below the horizon line as shown in Fig. 7-15.

Fig. 7-15

Front-lit shadow projection:
The LSVP is located below the horizon line and to the right of the RVP.

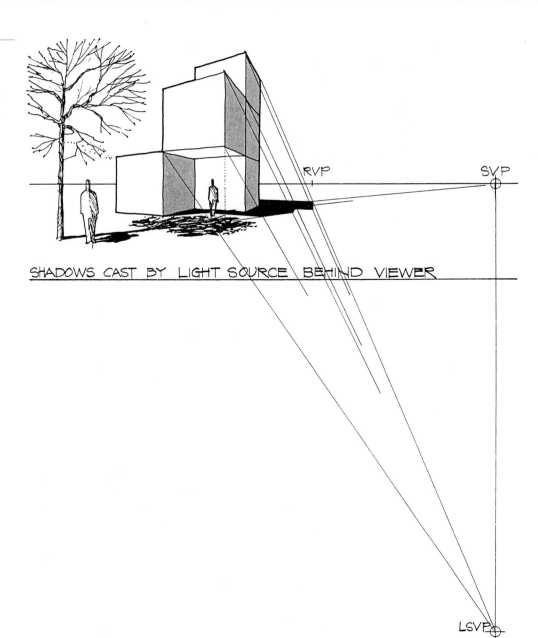

RVP   SVP

SHADOWS CAST BY LIGHT SOURCE BEHIND VIEWER

LSVP

Photographic and Video Projections

Slide and projection tracings

The direct tracing onto vellum of a projected image is an easy and versatile technique for producing a variety of different design drawings. This technique is most often applied to drawing perspective views of photographed models or projected photographs of an existing site or structure. The projection image is usually accomplished with a color slide projector or an overhead projector. In both cases, the projector is set up in a darkened room and the image is projected onto a tracing medium which has been attached to a smooth drawing surface.

The simplest means for accomplishing this arrangement is illustrated in Fig. 8-1, which shows the projector perpendicular to a wall-mounted drawing surface. A more elaborate arrangement using reflecting mirrors and a rear projection glass screen can be considered for a more permanent installation. The simple arrangement shown, however, is very versatile and can be used for most applications.

The projection machine should be set up on a sturdy stand or table, and its position should be marked with tape in case of accidental movement during the process.

Fig. 8-1

Color slide projection:
photo projection of color slides onto tracing vellum to produce perspective sketch of projected image. Models may be photographed within a pre-drawn grid to aid in future projection perspective.

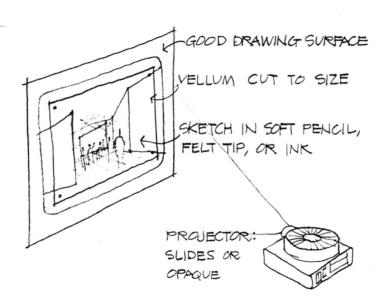

GOOD DRAWING SURFACE

VELLUM CUT TO SIZE

SKETCH IN SOFT PENCIL, FELT TIP, OR INK

PROJECTOR: SLIDES OR OPAQUE

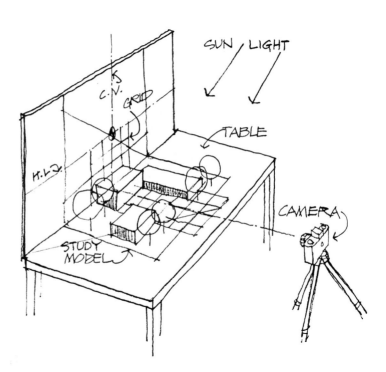

SUN / LIGHT

C.V. GRID

H.L.

TABLE

CAMERA

STUDY MODEL

Fig. 8-1 also illustrates a common "set-up" for photographing a rough study model, usually constructed of pressed or corrugated cardboard, and arranged on a table base which has been scribed with a grid drawn at the model scale. A background board also scribed by a grid is placed behind the model to act as a vertical scale reference. After development, the color slide transparency is projected and drawn in the manner described above, at the scale desired. Eye-level height and angle of vision can be accurately controlled by using a tripod and tape measure.[33]

Fig. 8-2

Oblique plan grid:
example of a plan grid photographed at an oblique angle to create a perspective ground plane grid, the vertical scale of which is determined by the ratio of the actual scale of a plan grid square and its corresponding square edge located in perspective. The actual plan grid square size is diminished by the percent of difference, and a vertical line is drawn at that particular point using the diminished value.

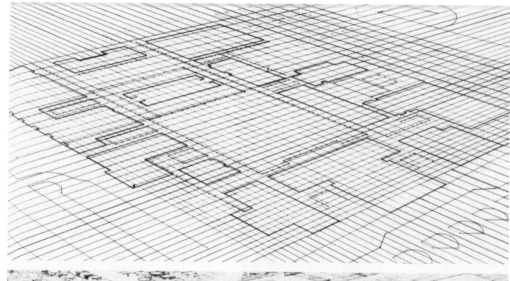

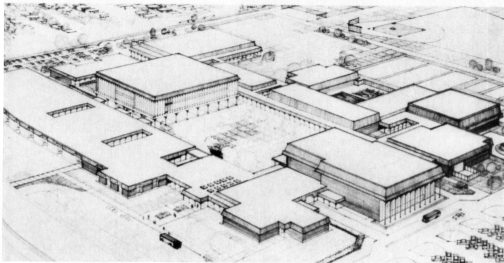

(Courtesy of Ernest Burden, from *Architectural Delineation: A Photographic Approach to Delineation*)

Plan grids

Perspective drawings can be generated from projected photographs of plans or scale models. Fig. 8-2 illustrates an application of a site grid photographed at an oblique angle to generate a naturally-diminished perspective ground plane showing the proposed plan layout; vertical scale is determined by using the ratio of the measured plan grid square side and the diminished side of a corresponding perspective grid square.[34] The vertical scale diminishes as the perspective grid squares diminish in size as follows: if the plan grid equals 10' (3m) and the particular perspective grid square edge measures 5' (1.5m), using the plan scale, then the vertical height will equal 50% 5/10 = .50) of the actual measured grid value, or 5' (1.5m) at that particular location on the perspective grid. A scale is used to measure a vertical line which measures 5' (1.5m) to represent a height of 10' (3m) in perspective.

Scale models

Another photographic projection method for producing a perspective drawing which is very supportive of design simulation analysis involves the photographing of simple scale models under controlled circumstances. Using a set-up similar to that illustrated in Fig. 8-1, models may be scribed with important vertical and horizontal grids, or reference lines, so that when photographed, a naturally-diminished sketch frame will result. Fig. 8-3 shows an example of such a procedure. It is recommended that a lens which yields a 45° cone of vision be used to avoid distortion found in wide angle lenses.[35] The tree, firetruck, and auto in Fig. 8-3 illustrates how placement of key scaling elements associated with the subject matter can be used as templates in the final sketch (note tree model in the final sketch).

Fig. 8-3

Perspective drawings from scale model photo-projections or enlargements:
The scale model has been photographed using scaling elements such as trees and vehicles to help determine scale in the final sketch.

(Courtesy of Ernest Burden, from *Architectural Delineation: A Photographic Approach to Presentation*)

Aerial photo overlays

Superimposing proposed development onto existing landscape views is another effective use of photo projection. This technique is more difficult than mere tracing of images. It requires that the perspective scale and horizon line location be determined by carefully studying the photograph for known dimensions such as surveying section lines, widths of roads, bridges, structures, etc. After the critical points have been located, a grid is drawn over the photograph and the proposed design is laid out. Fig. 8-4 is a drawing produced from such a slide projection and illustrates a proposed design concept from an aerial viewpoint. The existing farmland is shown to be preserved, and proposed condominiums are shown clustered about its periphery. The chief scaling element in the photograph was the existing roadway which is expressed in the drawing, slightly re-aligned.

Fig. 8-4

Aerial view of farmland showing proposed development superimposed onto slide image.
Existing roadway and farm fields were used to establish scale within the photograph prior to super-imposition.

Photographic and electrostatic processes

Electrostatic photo reproduction is a cost-effective tool for reproducing drawings, photographs, and sketches for the purpose of creating design simulation drawings in the early stages of design. Using this process, line drawings can be easily reduced or enlarged and printed on reproducible tracing vellum, which can in turn be used to make reproducible base sheets with reasonable accuracy. Small thumbnail sketches may be rapidly enlarged to serve as preliminary concept presentation drawings, or as templates for larger, more finished presentation drawings.

A variation of this process is the direct printing of 35 mm. color slides using either color electrostatic enlargements or color laser enlargements. These enlargements may be augmented using photo drawing techniques to show "before and after" sketches.

Video capture and computer imaging processes

Videotape recording and playback units provide a unique form of graphic assistance. They provide direct viewing of scale models for design assessments and for "stop frame" sketching, or direct photographing of the video image for later projection sketching. Although the equipment is initially expensive, the potential of this technique for aiding design process and design drawing is very high.

Capturing video images has been enhanced by computer systems that scan video images, and allow electronic editing so that proposed designs may be superimposed onto "captured" existing conditions images. Although not a drawing system in the classical sense, it does provide an extraordinary way to visually simulate spatial and visual aspects of proposed designs.[36]

The techniques and tools presented in this chapter represent a cross-section of basic photographic and imaging processes that are readily accessible and easy to use. More detailed information can be acquired by referring to the cited references in the Bibliography.

Computer-Aided
Landscape Perspective

The computer has altered professional design work in both practical and theoretical ways. While computers in offices are increasingly being used to draft production drawings, to analyze design programs, and to assist in other phases of design and planning work, we are also expanding our inquiry of how the design mind organizes, visualizes, and manipulates design data.[37] Much of this inquiry is fueled by research in artificial intelligence and the design of expert systems. The resultant technology touches almost every aspect of our professional lives. This book, for example, was written and its type was set using a word processor, and the entire book manuscript is contained on a single diskette.[38]

CAD and Conceptual Design Visualization

Researchers, including this author, are seeking ways to integrate the computer more directly and "unselfconsciously" into the conceptual or creative design development phase of our work with the aim of improving accuracy, broadening the knowledge base of physical design, and increasing the efficiency and reliability of design assessment. At present, about ninety per cent of computer applications in design offices are for production drawings and related documents, leaving the "creative act of design" virtually unaided by computers.[39]

It is therefore ironic that a chapter on Computer-Aided Design (CAD) be included in a book about drawing and visualizing space. In the same manner that early attempts to create mathematically correct perspective were met with outrage by the seventeenth century painters of the French court (see Introduction), current experiments with artificial intelligence and expert systems are greeted with suspicion by designers who have been trained in the tradition of modern architecture and landscape architecture. In fairness, it must be stated that the state-of-the-art of CAD as it applies to creative design within ill-defined problem sets is still in its infancy, and appears to be an alien and unfriendly environment for most designers. As we approach the close of the twentieth century, the irony is further compounded by the resurgence of an interest in design drawings as works of individual art (visualizations), rather than as a means for simulating and realizing the built form. The means are beginning to become more important than the ends.[40]

■ *As we are capable of producing "perfectly drawn" images by machine, there is a coincident interest in the fine art of drawing in styles that border on the impressionistic.*

This chapter, therefore, is meant to serve as a bridge between traditional design drawing and a total CAD environment to demonstrate how the computer may be used as a tool for visualization without abandoning basic and traditional design processes or human perceptual insights.

Computer Drawn Space Grids

Figs. 9-1 to 9-9 were produced using AutoCAD,™ and represent an attempt to create an electronic sketch environment for producing the type of perspective construction space grids which were produced by hand in the preceding chapters.[41] The purpose of these images is to illustrate how a computer environment may be adapted to allow for more designer-machine interaction. All of the space grid images exist within a menu-driven environment and have been programmed to calculate the area of a designated space, the spatial coordinates of a selected point, or the distances from the viewer to any inserted object or point in space.[42]

The system uses the direct drawing approach and eliminates the need for a plan view. In fact, the main purpose of the system is to allow for three-dimensional images to be explored very rapidly during the conceptual design phase. The system can be described as being an electronic set of "perspective charts" that are always available to the designer.

Once a perspective view is chosen, menu-driven entourage items may be placed within the perspective view using a cursor, and the item will appear as it would be seen from the distance indicated on the space grid. The purpose of this system is to generate perspective images of spatial ideas as they develop early in the design process, using fragmentary information in a visually-precise environment, without an expenditure of great amounts of time or energy.

Fig. 9-1

One-point perspective view angle menu:
Each icon creates an enlarged perspective chart for the view selected.

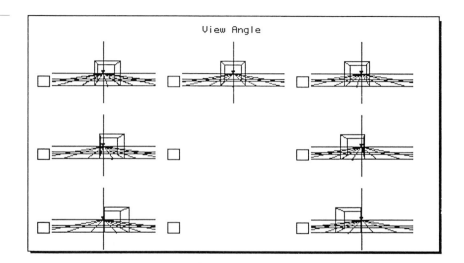

Fig. 9-2

Two-point perspective view angle menu:
The icons represent 20/70°, 30/60°, and 45/45° perspective views with options for left or right CV orientations.

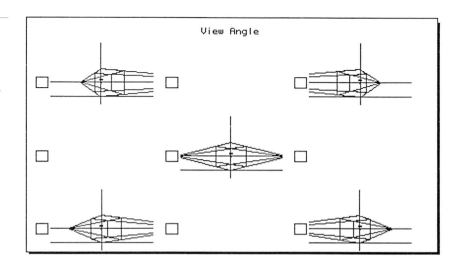

Fig. 9-3

Three-point perspective view angle menu:
The icons represent various views of the three-point base cube as the cube is rotated in space.

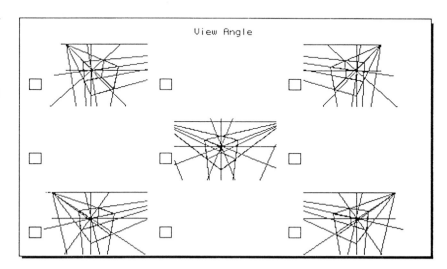

Figs. 9-1 to 9-3 represent screen menus for one-, two-, and three-point perspective views and if selected, will produce screen images such as those seen in Figs. 9-4 to 9-6.

Fig. 9-4

One-point perspective space grid:
The grid shows depth lines, and divides the ground line into 1' (0.25m) increments for ease of scaling and construction. All scaling increments may be proportionally increased or decreased. The circles represent 30° and 60° cones of vision.

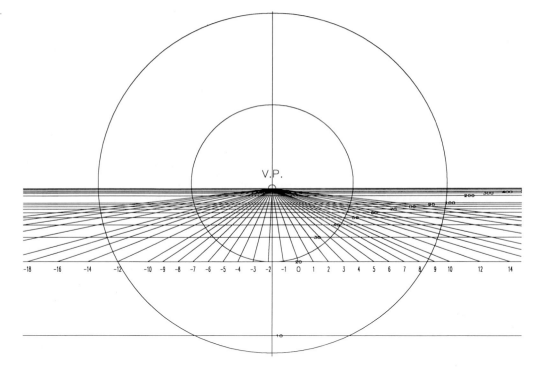

Fig. 9-5

Two-point perspective space grid:
The grid is divided into 10' (3m) squares and numbers have been suppressed. The LMP, CV, RMP, and RVP are located for construction purposes.

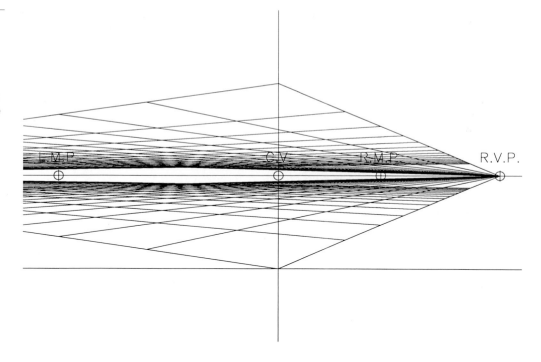

Fig. 9-6

Three-point perspective space grid:
The grid is divided into equal units and can be assigned any value to achieve the desired scale (see Chapter 5).

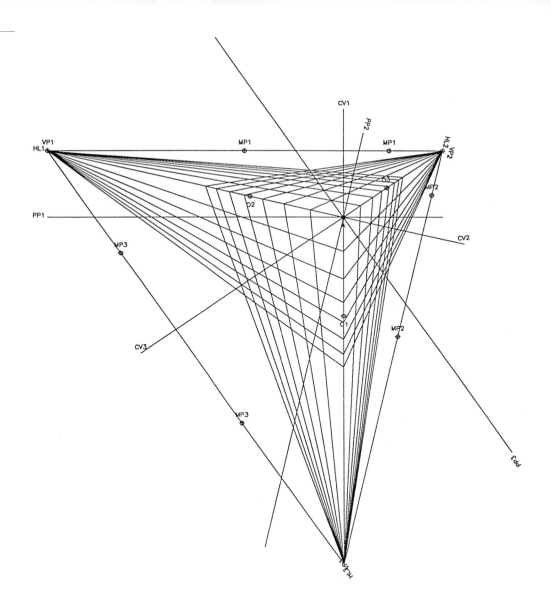

Fig. 9-4 illustrates one of the selected menu views for one-point perspective. This view shows the VP centered slightly to the left of the ground plane grid centerline. The depth lines are labeled and distances to the left (-) and to the right (+) are indicated in one foot (0.25m) increments. The eye-level height is 5' (1.5m) but is adjustable as a menu choice. The designer may designate the grid increments. Figs. 9-5 and 9-6 show comparable sketch frames for two-point and three-point views.

A sketch is created by inserting entourage items from various menus illustrated by Figs. 9-7 and 9-8. Additional menu items such as vehicles, small structures, etc., may be created by the designer to enrich the vocabulary of the preliminary sketch.

Fig. 9-7

People menu:
Each person may be inserted into a one-, two-, or three-point perspective space grid using a cursor and will be sized automatically to match the appropriate landscape depth and viewer height values (see Fig. 9-9).

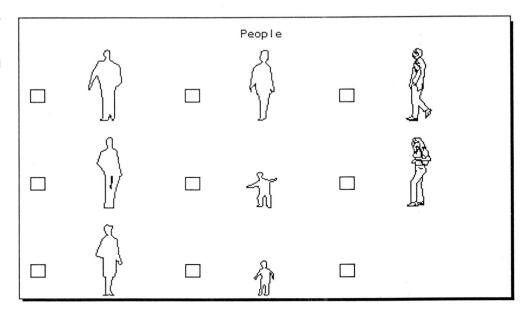

Fig. 9-8

Tree and shrub menu:
Each tree or shrub may be inserted into any space grid and will be automatically sized according to the particular view selected. Each plant receives a co-ordinate point value for conversion to a plan view of the constructed perspective view.

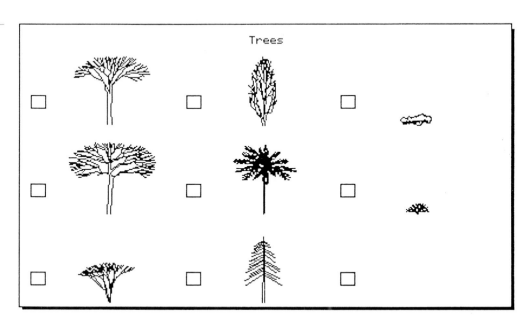

Fig. 9-9

Two-point landscape perspective showing people, plants, and implied landscape space:
The output options include grid suppression for a pure line-drawing effect. Spatial elements may be converted to a plan view to test the layout pattern implied by the perspective view. This simple program does not include hidden line removal.

R.V.P.

Fig. 9-9 illustrates a two-point perspective view showing the addition of people, trees, and shrubs selected from the menus. The co-ordinates and the distance from the viewer of each entered object is calculated and stored as a data base simply by locating the object within the the sketch frame using the cursor in the same manner that plan data is digitized. It is now possible to generate a plan view of the perspective just created. This capability achieves a primary objective of this book, which is to encourage the use of perspective images to generate plan implications rather than working exclusively in plan view first and perspective view second.

A space frame so constructed could be printed on a small laser printer, and photographically or electrostatically enlarged to serve as a large format sketch frame for more detailed rendering and drawing. If the computer system is equipped with a high resolution plotter, or a large format laser printer, the enlarging process could occur within the computer, and the photo process would be eliminated.

■ *The speed with which these images are created makes them very useful during initial conceptual design phases, because they offer immediate visual feedback to ideas in their formative stage without disrupting the flow of work or thought.*

It is in this way that a truly interactive CAD environment should operate in conceptual design work phases. The designer's internal flow of thinking should not be disrupted. The computer should represent an electronic "felt marking pen," and its pull-down menu features should allow all calculations to be done by the machine, so that the designer may see and evaluate the consequences of a choice immediately after its selection.

The software for the drawing program illustrations was specially designed for this book, but it demonstrates the capability of computer-assisted visualization for aiding the very heart of the design process in a manner that resembles the "normal" designer working pattern. It also points to the fact that each office may be capable of customizing any number of specialized design drawing systems to satisfy particular client group needs, or unique intra-office requirements.

Advanced Computer Simulation

The work shown in Figs. 9-10 to 9-22 represents a more sophisticated use of current technology by the landscape architecture firm, Design Workshop Inc., of Denver, Colorado. This firm, which has special capabilities in landscape planning and urban design, is an example of a growing number of design offices which use the computer to simulate design and planning decisions during the creative process as well as during the production and presentation processes.[43]

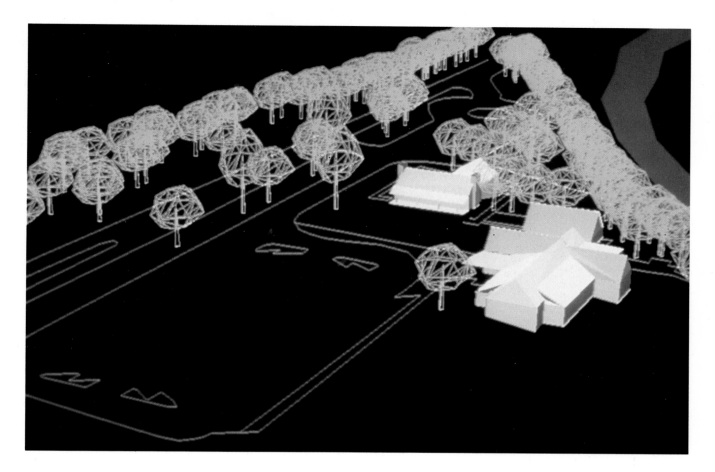

Fig. 9-10

Aerial perspective computer image of a proposed National Park Visitor's Center:
The perspective view has been generated from a digitized layout plan of the proposed design.

Fig. 9-11

Video view of proposed construction site:
A video frame of the site has been converted to a digitized computer image and will be "painted" upon to simulate the proposed construction.

Figs. 9-10 to 9-12 show the application of a video capture system that superimposes a three-dimensional computer image of a proposed National Park Visitor's Center onto a stored video frame of the proposed site. Fig. 9-10 is an aerial view of site layout derived from a digitized plan.

Fig. 9-12

View of proposed construction superimposed upon the video frame: The CAD image in Fig. 9-10 has been painted onto the existing site to simulate post-construction conditions. The sun angle has been adjusted to match the video image altitude and azimuth for a realistic shadow pattern effect.

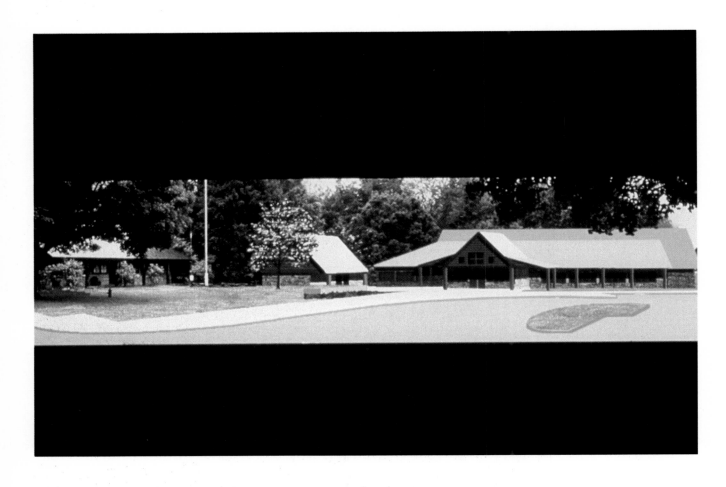

Figs. 9-13 to 9-22 were developed for the proposed new town of Summerlin, Nevada, a project of Howard Hughes Properties.

Figs. 9-13 to 9-15 demonstrate the use of a wireframe base drawing to execute a more traditional-appearing finished drawing as illustrated in Fig. 9-15. The wireframe drawing in Fig. 9-13 and the solid modeling drawing in Fig. 9-14 were generated by the computer from a digitized plan. In essence, the CAD system is serving as a customized perspective chart or sketch frame to create an image of a proposed village center in a new community.

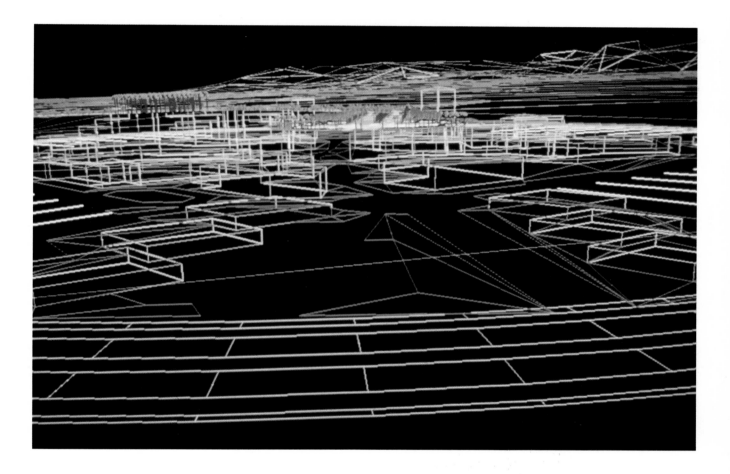

Fig. 9-13

Wireframe image of proposed new community village center:
The drawing shows the essential elements of a perspective drawing rendered in a wireframe style with no hidden line removal. Buildings, roads, and topographic features are indicated.

Fig. 9-14

Solid model image of the proposed village center:
All visible surfaces have been made opaque to add clarity to the image in Fig. 9-13. The drawing can now serve as a template for a conventional hand-drawn image.

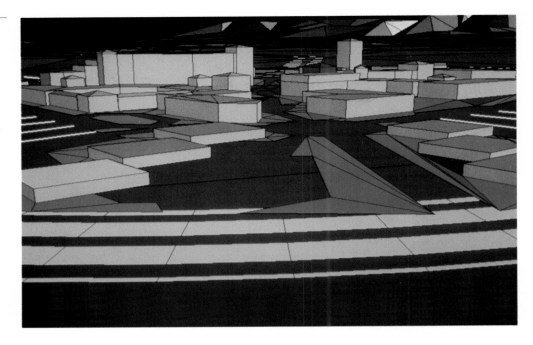

Fig. 9-15

Hand-drawn perspective image of proposed village center:
The proposed landscape development plan has been superimposed upon the computer image to create an accurate preliminary design of the new proposal.

Figs. 9-16 to 9-17 demonstrate the use of wireframe images to assess various versions of a design proposal. Fig. 9-16 shows one design option for a residential development in a wireframe format. Fig. 9-17 shows a rendered overlay study of another design option for the same development site.

Fig. 9-16

Wireframe image of a proposed residential development:
An image showing structures, major trees, and roads.

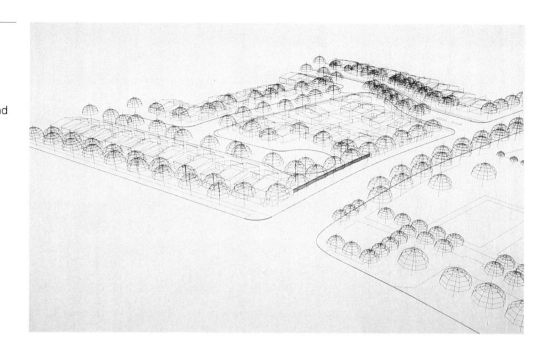

Fig. 9-17

Hand-rendered perspective over a wireframe image:
This drawing represents another alternative for the proposed residential development shown in Fig. 9-16, and illustrates how several versions of a design may be tested very rapidly.

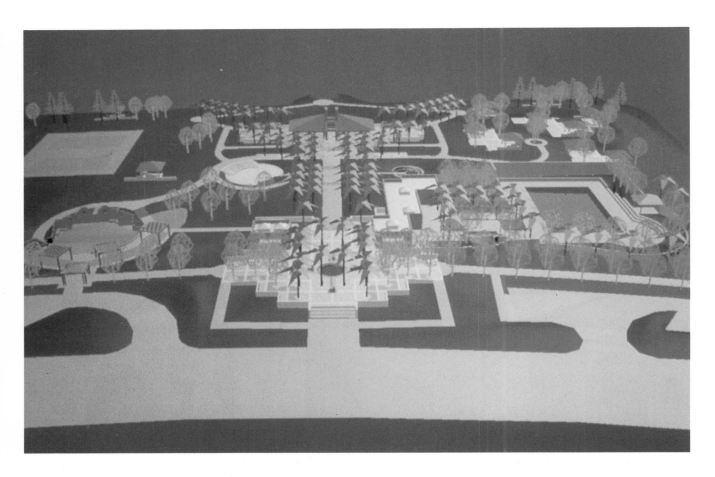

Figs. 9-18 to 9-22 represent a "pure" computer simulation of a proposed neighborhood park in a new community. To simplify data entry and image clarity, only major design elements such as buildings, park structures, roads, walks, and large trees are drawn. The sequence of drawings illustrates how a proposed design can be totally explored using zooming and eye-level functions. If such an electronic tour occurs during the design development phase, corrections in layout, proportioning, massing, etc., may be made before the design is completed. Special attention should be paid to Figs. 9-21 and 9-22 because they explore the human eye-level experience of the potential viewer.

■ *Research has shown that the eye-level landscape perspective view in CAD simulation is more effective for discovering design errors than are the more traditional aerial perspective views.*[44]

Fig. 9-19

Oblique detail of park pool area:
The simulation system allows viewers to take a complete aerial tour of the park as if they were flying in a helicopter.

In Chapter 3, Figs. 3-11 and 3-12 illustrate precisely the type of animation that can be easily achieved in a CAD environment. Simulation tools such as those presented in this entire book, and Chapter 9 specifically, can increase our ability to more accurately predict the physical qualities of a proposed design.

Fig. 9-20

Oblique detail of gathering site:
Subtle ground-plane undulations are indicated through shading.

Fig. 9-21

Eye-level view of the gathering area:
The system allows the viewer to walk through the site and to literally follow all pedestrian paths to check for unforeseen errors in the design.

Fig. 9-22

Eye-level view of the pavilion arrival area:
To create a more realistic view, additional elements such as shrubs, people, cars, and small scale site improvements could be added to these close-up views. However, to save time and computer memory, only the most obvious elements are simulated.

Conclusion

"Drawing space" is a central skill required of any profession which has as its main purpose the planning and design of places and spaces for human habitation and enjoyment. But more fundamental than this skill is the intellectual ability to mentally create spaces and to ascribe to them physical attributes, proportions and dimensions, functional objectives, and most importantly, behavioral potentials. Such a design problem setting is clearly of the ill-defined, or "wicked" category, and requires acknowledgement of "unknown unknowns" and "leaps of faith" as well.[45]

Simulating the consequences of physical design changes, or altered states, becomes all the more compelling. This book offers a method for simulating the three-dimensional spatial effects of design in landscape settings, and suggests a range of tools which if applied in concert, may be useful in assessing both the simulations per se, and important aspects of the design itself.

However, the "content" of a proposed design is only partially addressed by merely drawing its physical and spatial properties. Any system of drawing used for design assessment, regardless of method, should be tempered by the knowledge that all physical design, besides having a visual consequence, also affects and is affected by cultural values and behavioral expectations, semiotic content, economics, ecological systems, political processes, etc., to name an important few.[46]

It is therefore imperative that our drawings of space, and the designs that we propose for reshaping it, be as accurate as possible so that their narrowly-defined role may be fully realized. We who are responsible for producing the designs should make every effort to explore ways that will make us more effective in understanding our own work, and in illustrating its conceptual and practical content to others.

Annotated Bibliography

Arnheim, Rudolf: *Visual Thinking*, University of California Press, Berkeley and Los Angeles, 1969. An essential book for designers who draw on paper what they see inside of their heads. It suggests a holistic model for analytical and perceptual thinking.

Burden, Ernest: *Architectural Delineation: A Photograhic Approach to Presentation*, McGraw-Hill Book Co., New York, 1971. An excellent advanced text for executing both in-process design studies and highly refined presentation renderings using photographic shortcuts.

Burden, Ernest: *Entourage: A Tracing File for Architecture and Interior Design*, McGraw-Hill Book Co., New York, 1981. A valuable portfolio of tracing elements, with advice on composition and view selection.

Coulin, Claudius: *Step-by-Step Perspective Drawing for Architects, Draftsmen, and Designers*, Van Nostrand Reinhold Co., New York, 1966. An indispensable teaching text for basic, clearly-illustrated perspective construction with special emphasis on shadow projection methods.

Ching, Francis D. K.: *Architectural Graphics*, Van Nostrand Reinhold Co., New York, 1974. An excellent introductory text on drafting and basic architectural drawing, with emphasis on processes and technique in well-illustrated, clearly-stated language.

Ching, Francis D. K.: *Architecture: Form, Space, and Order*, Van Nostrand Reinhold Co., New York, 1979. Essential for any student of design because it organizes spatial concepts very clearly, and illustrates them with beautifully-drawn, historically-important examples of built works.

Descargues, Pierre: *Perspective*, Harry N. Abrams, Inc., New York, 1977. A rich display of prints depicting early experiments with perspective from the sixteenth through the nineteenth centuries, concisely translated from French in spare, but informative language.

Doblin, Jay: *Perspective: A New System for Designers*, Watson-Guptill Publications, New York, 1957. A highly idiosyncratic, but very creative and useful approach to perspective drawing, with several innovative suggestions and shortcuts.

Doyle, Michael E.: *Color Drawing*, Van Nostrand Reinhold Co., New York, 1981. This book addresses color applied to design drawing in a clear, effective format. It also provides examples that are cross-disciplinary, and is useful to both beginning and advanced students.

Evans, Larry: *Architectural Illustration Guides*, Vol. 2, Instant Landscape, San Francisco, 1972. A general portfolio of tracing elements, but noted for its elementary instruction of drawing composition and other useful production hints.

Hall, Edward T.: *The Hidden Dimension*, Doubleday and Company, New York, 1966. A classic work on culture, space, perception, and behavior that has influenced a broad spectrum of disciplines, including political science, ethology, architecture, design, and others. It is important as a derivative source for cultural data for designers.

Lockard, William Kirby: *Design Drawing Experiences*, 4th edition, Pepper Press, Tucson, 1979. An excellent basic drawing and design process book, fully illustrated by clearly-drawn examples.

Lockard, William Kirby: *Design Drawing*, Van Nostrand Reinhold Co., New York, 1982. This is a definitive work on design drawing as a process of thought and action, and makes a compelling presentation through well-documented text, and clear informative drawings and photographs.

Lynch, Kevin and Gary Hack: *Site Planning*, 3rd edition, MIT Press, Cambridge, 1984. Although not a drawing book, it contains design and planning theory which supports drawing content and design element relationships.

Martin, Leslie C.: *Design Graphics*, 2nd edition, MacMillan, Inc., New York, 1968. A fundamental text on drafting, lettering, perspective, and projections.

McCartney, T.O.: *Precision Perspective Drawing*, McGraw-Hill Book Co., New York, 1963. An advanced book on perspective construction covering wide-angle construction, with emphasis on determining the size and perspective view of a drawing based on the the optics (focal length) of the person or group viewing the finished rendering.

Muller, Edward J.: *Architectural Drawing and Light Construction*, 2nd edition, Prentice-Hall, Inc. Englewood Cliffs, 1976. A basic architectural drafting primer.

Porter, Tom et. al.: *Manual of Graphic Technique*, Vols., 1, 2, 3, and 4, Charles Scribner's Sons, New York, 1980-87. Basic to advanced illustrations of a vast array of techniques and suggestions for a full range of drawing types, useful to the design student in general.

Rowe, Peter G.: *Design Thinking*, MIT Press, Cambridge, 1987. Although primarily concerned with design thinking as it relates to architecture, this book provides a very useful structure for general design thinking and inquiry, with well-documented case studies to support the main ideas.

Szabo, Marc: *Drawing File for Architects, Illustrators, and Designers*, Van Nostrand Reinhold Co., New York, 1976. A portfolio of professional tracing templates used for perspective rendering, with useful hints about composition and execution.

Walters, Nigel V. and John Bromham: *Principles of Perspective*, Watson-Guptill Publications, New York, 1974. A concise and beautifully illustrated treatise on descriptive geometry without reference to a particular discipline or profession, showing many shortcut and advanced methods useful to many types of designers.

Wang, Thomas C.: *Plan and Section Drawing*, Van Nostrand Reinhold Co., New York, 1979. The techniques shown are very specific to landscape architecture and site planning, but it is very useful as a basic drawing text.

Zion, Robert: *Trees for Architecture*, Reinhold Publishing Co., New York, 1968. A photographic essay of trees in four seasons, useful for studying structure, form, and foliage effects of selected trees.

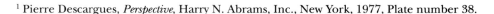

Footnotes

[1] Pierre Descargues, *Perspective*, Harry N. Abrams, Inc., New York, 1977, Plate number 38.

[2] Ernest Burden, *Entourage: A Tracing File for Architecture and Interior Design.* McGraw-Hill Book Co., New York, 1981.

[3] Mark S. Lindhult and Nicholas T. Dines, "Perspective Sketching with Microcomputers," *Landscape Architecture*, July/August, 1985. pp. 56-57.

[4] Mark S. Lindhult, "Redefining Professional Roles in the CAD Era," *Landscape Architecture*, July/August, 1988. p. 128.

[5] Pierre Descargues, *ibid.*, p. 9.

[6] Pierre Descargues, *ibid.*

[7] John Ives Sewall, *A History of Western Art*, Henry Holt and Company, New York, 1953, p. 855. See Figs. 18.12 and 18.13.

[8] Geoffrey and Susan Jellicoe, et. al., *The Oxford Companion to Gardens*, Oxford University Press, New York, 1986, pp. 56-57.

[9] Gordon Cullen, *Townscape*, Reinhold Publishing Co., New York, 1961.

[10] Christopher Alexander, *A Pattern Language*, Oxford University Press, New York,; Jon Lang, "A Model of the Designing Process," *Designing for Human Behavior*, Dowden, Hutchinson, and Ross, Inc., Stroudsburg, Pa., 1974, pp. 45-46.

[11] Kevin Lynch and Gary Hack, *Site Planning*, 3rd edition, MIT Press, Cambridge, 1984. See Chapter 5.

[12] *Op. cit.,* Lang, p. 44.

[13] Mark S. Lindhult and Nicholas T. Dines, "Creativity in CAD: A Convergence of Ideas", International Conference on Engineering Design, Scientific Society of Mechanical Engineers, Budapest, Hungary (abstract), 1988.

[14] This process is patterned after Lang's "Model of the Designing Process."

[15] Francis D. K. Ching, *Architectural Graphics*, Van Nostrand Reinhold, New York, 1975. (See additional descriptions of drawing types.)

[16] *Op. cit.,* Lynch and Hack.

[17] *Op. cit.,* Descargues, Plates 47, 81, 148.

[18] T. O. McCartney, *Precision Perspective Drawing*, McGraw-Hill Book Co., New York, 1963, p. 177, Fig. 8-4.

[19] Kevin Lynch, *Image of the City*, Technology Press and Harvard University Press, Cambridge, 1960.

[20] *Op. cit.,* McCartney, p. 6, Figs. 1-4 and 1-5.

[21] *Op. cit.,* Descargues, Plate 38.

[22] Gordon Cullen, *Townscape*, Reinhold Publishing Co., New York, 1961.

[23] Nigel Walters and John Bromham, *Principles of Perspective*, Watson-Guptill Publications, New York, 1974, p. 95.

[24] Jay Doblin, *Perspective: A New System for Designers*, Watson-Guptill Publications, New York, 1956.

[25] *Op. cit.,* Walters and Bromham, p. 27.

[26] *Ibid.,* p. 91.

[27] Francis D. K. Ching, *Architectural Graphics*, Van Nostrand Reinhold Co., New York, 1975, pp. 30-33.

[28] Kevin Lynch, *Image of the City*, Technology Press and Harvard University Press, Cambridge, 1960. Thresholds of spatial enclosure and loss of enclosure.

[29] Sketch is a facsimile of a technique used by Johnson and Roy, Ann Arbor, Michigan.

[30] *Op. cit.,* Walters and Bromham, pp. 122-124.

[31] *Ibid.,* p. 62.

[32] Sources used for shadow construction are: Claudius Coulin, *Step-by-Step Perspective Drawing*, Van Nostrand Reinhold, New York, 1966; Leslie Martin, *Design Graphics*, 2nd edition, MacMillan Inc., New York, 1968; *Op. cit.,* Walters and Bromham.

[33] Ernest Burden, *Architectural Delineation: A Photographic Approach to Presentation*, McGraw-Hill Book Co., New York, 1971.

[34] *Ibid.,* p. 41.

[35] *Ibid.,* p. 65.

[36] Brian Orland, "Video Imaging: A Powerful Tool for Visualization and Analysis," *Landscape Architecture*, Vol. 78, No. 5, July/August, 1988, pp. 78-88.

[37] Peter G. Rowe, *Design Thinking*, MIT Press, Cambridge, 1987.

[38] The manuscript was typed using Microsoft Word on a Macintosh II (a registered trademark of the Apple Computer Corporation), and the layout was composed using Pagemaker (a registered trademark of Aldus Corporation).

[39] Op. *cit.,* Lindhult, *Landscape Architecture*, July/August, 1988.

[40] Gordon Brown and Mark Gelernter, "Education: Veering from Practice," *Progressive Architecture*, March, 1989, pp. 61-66.

[41] AutoCAD is a registered trademark of Autodesk, Inc.

[42] The software was developed by Ms. Fang Fang, who at the time was a Landscape Architecture graduate student and research associate at the University of Massachusetts.

[43] For more information on Design Workshop Inc., and the technical specifications of the computer equipment and software used to produce the work illustrated, see Land*scape Architecture,* April, 1990, Vol. 80, No. 4, pp. 72-75.

[44] Unpublished discussion with John Danahy of the Centre for Landscape Research, University of Toronto, during a demonstration of real-time design simulation of various urban design projects, 1988.

[45] Herbert A. Simon, "The Structure of Ill-structured Problems," *Artificial Intelligence-4*, North Holland Publishing Company, 1973, pp. 181-201.

[46] Barrie Greenbie, *Spaces: Dimensions of the Human Landscape*, Yale University Press, New Haven, 1987.

Index

(Because basic terms are repeated so often throughout the text, indexed words and phrases have been limited to primary descriptions and elaborations, with illustrations indicated by bold type.)

About the Author

Nicholas T. Dines, ASLA, is a member of the American Society of Landscape Architects and is an associate professor and the former director of the Master of Landscape Architecture Program at the University of Massachusetts, Amherst. He teaches courses in studio design, construction technology, design graphics, design theory, and professional practice.

A graduate of Michigan State University and the Harvard University Graduate School of Design, Professor Dines has offered national seminars for the ASLA on energy-efficient site design, and served as visiting professor of landscape construction for five years at the Harvard Graduate School of design. He has more than 23 years of experience in public and private sector design and construction, and is the co-editor of *Time-Saver Standards for Landscape Architecture* for McGraw-Hill Inc., which received an ASLA Merit Award for design communication.

Professor Dines continues to work with colleagues at the University of Massachusetts to develop methods to more closely integrate computer applications into the actual work of design, and is currently writing a book about spatial aspects of landscape design theory. He lives in Williamsburg, Massachusetts where he maintains a design consulting office.